A Leap of Faith

(25 days at the Mercy Seat)

By
Dr Deborah Starczewski

www.xulonpress.com

CONTENTS

Contents

Foreword by Dr. Rick Ross

**Dr. Rick Ross --Lead Pastor
CONCORD FIRST ASSEMBLY
Assemblies of God, Assistant Superintendent,
North Carolina**

It is a joy to see Deborah thriving in her abilities and gifted-
ness as she communicates hope to everyone she meets. I
have known Deborah and Dan Starczewski for nine years and
they are faithful to the call of Christ on their lives. She teaches
weekly at our home church, Concord First Assembly in
Concord, NC and infuses people with faith and holy boldness.

The miraculous story you will read about in this book
shows the detail that God goes to in order to reveal His
agenda and design for the life of His children. It is also a
story of encouragement and the part that the body of Christ
plays in the midst of struggles and trials.

The condition of the heart of man is multifaceted and
this particular story of her husband, Dan, and his process of
healing will keep you turning another page as the miraculous
story unfolds through her style of writing. You will see just
how God is into the details and reveals what He is doing
when we choose to turn aside to observe.

Deborah draws beautiful illustrations from the physical
things that God puts in her path to confirm what He had
already been whispering into her spirit. Her writing inevitably
urges all of God's children to be spiritually aware, listen to

God, pay attention to His promptings, and then, obey!

Her command and recall of scripture sets her apart from many other believers and the Word of God that flows from her instills hope and confidence as we journey through our circumstances. Be encouraged as you read and also take a leap of faith to believe in Jesus, as He is our only hope!

--Dr. Rick Ross, Lead Pastor,
Concord First Assembly, Concord, NC
Assemblies of God, Assistant Superintendent,
North Carolina

Foreword by Dr. Neal Speight

When I met Deborah eleven years ago, little did I know just how profound her influence would be in my life. With the exception of my mom, no woman has moved the direction of my life toward the Lord more significantly than this dear friend. As a result of obedience in the midst of her experiences, I believe God has filled Deborah with wisdom that we would all do well to take to heart.

I have had the privilege of watching one of God's greatest servants lead by example. Being obedient to God's call, she has displayed the fruit of a truly spirit-filled life. He sent her to my office for medical care. At least, that's what I thought. I came to realize that as with so many others, God sent Deborah to minister to *me*. As the years unfolded, time and time again I saw her speak into my life and into the lives of others either wisdom from the Word or a direct revelation from His heart to ours. When we listened we were blessed, and when we did not, God made it clear the consequences of disobedience.

Without a doubt, knowing Deborah has been one of the most supernatural experiences of my life. From the interpretations of dreams, to the decision to marry, from direction in my career, to long-distance travel, the Lord has used her to confirm what I already knew and at times turn me around when I refused to follow Him. I thank God for her obedience and her presence through these years, for had she not listened to the Lord she would have never called to warn of upcoming events in my life, or interpret dreams that unfolded just as she said. Through the practice of her faith, she has allowed me to see that God does indeed care intimately about what happens in all of our lives. What a delightful journey it has been.

In her first book, *God's Priceless Treasure*, you find the wisdom of one tried by fire and who has earned the right to speak because of her obedience and devotion to the God of creation. I encourage you to read every word and let them warm your heart as they have mine. Deborah's second book, *A LEAP OF FAITH*, will open your eyes to the details of God's divine intervention on many levels. HE is using Deborah to teach people to run to Jesus and to the Mercy Seat daily. I am again amazed at the level of "miraculous coincidence" that occurs in this woman's life and in those for whom she cares. I believe God is using her to help lead others into this favor the Lord wants for all of us as we choose to obey His Word.

To my dearest friend I say thank you for your service and for imparting these precious words of wisdom to us all and for teaching us to take a *leap of faith* and dare to trust God in every situation. I can never repay you for what you have done in my life through your service to Him.

--Neal Speight
The Center for Wellness, Dr. Neal Speight,
Matthews North Carolina

Acknowledgments

On a drive home from Charlotte, Mother and I were talking about this new book, A LEAP OF FAITH. We reflected on God's divine intervention in my husband's life, and the fact many have said this book will be a New York Times Best seller giving glory to God.

As we approached the next light just before the freeway, there was a black SUV with a bumper sticker: IT'S IN THE BOOK. I stay amazed at how God confirms His Word and makes us acutely aware of His divine presence in our lives.

Did you know that *it's all in THE BOOK—The Bible?* The Word of God has the answer to every question and every problem you will ever face in life. God's principles are wisdom and *when we obey God,* we can live in His blessing! The events you will read about in *this* book will open your eyes to believe God for yourself and have hope again!

While at an appointment, God positioned a nurse in my life to tell me I needed to be on every talk show and in every pulpit across the nations sharing this amazing story to give everyone hope again! I had to reschedule this appointment five different times so she was curious as to what was going on in my life. As I shared the short version of this amazing story, tears began to flow from her eyes down on her laptop. She stopped and looked at me and shared her heart for me to tell this story! Thank you to this nurse for being an inspiration!

As always, the completion of any project like this is never the work of just the author. I am deeply indebted to the **Holy**

Spirit and my family and friends for their help:

To my precious husband Dan who God raised up for "such a time as this" to do His Kingdom work with me. I love you sweetheart! God divinely put us together in marriage and ministry. Thank you for your faithful support and for partnering with me to do what God has called us to do together.

To my mother Shirley Rush who is the epitome of love and faithfulness and the gift that she is from God as the greatest mother a person could ever have...for her continued prayer support and help in the ministry, and for our entire family.

To our dear friends Dr. Rick and Susan Ross, for their faithful support and encouragement...for standing beside us in the good times and the tough times—a true friend is born for adversity.

Thank you to our family, many friends and family of God for standing with us through prayer, petitions, and many visits as we walked through this journey of life and death circumstances. To Dr. James Bower (Dan's cardiologist): Thank you for standing with us and for your genuine concern as you walked through this journey with us. God has placed a great calling on your life. Thank you for standing with us and for such great care! Thank you to your wife for her support... as behind every great man is a great wife.

To Dan's heart surgeon for his faithfulness to his calling and for his faithfulness in walking through this journey with us for the sake of my husband's life. Thank you to Sanger Heart and Mercy Hospital staff. Thank you to Dr, Neal Speight and all the other medical staff God positioned with us at Mercy Hospital.

There is no way I can mention every person by name—so I say "thank you" to all of you! God knows you all by name! To all of you I say a deeply felt thank you!

Deborah Starczewski

INTRODUCTION

One morning I woke up after listening to my husband's cough become increasingly worse and prayed a strange prayer. I told the Lord I was aggravated and didn't want to be a widow. I asked God to speak to Dan for it was obvious he was ignoring my warnings.

I would wake up during the night and see my husband in an open-vision like a corpse. I knew we had a serious problem. Then God gave me a dream about a four sided clear plexi-glass piece of equipment that surrounded me with a fountain of liquid in a beautiful color of purple that seemed to go through the clouds, passing through the heavens to the Mercy Seat. Don't ask me how I knew that—I just knew. It was like God was depositing hope and insight straight into my life in a unique way that all might not understand—at first.

From admission on February 24th to leaving the hospital on the first day of Spring, God showed Himself strong on behalf of Dan! Dan went into heart failure on February 24th, but God gave us our own resurrection story with many divine interventions that saved his life. I told Dan that God had given him a new lease on life. God made Himself strong on Dan's behalf with a witness of His resurrection power. God cares about us! He cares about you too! He cares about life and all the details. All the dots seem to connect when you take the time to actually observe.

If you have lost hope or wonder if God sees your situation, you will have hope again in the one and only God who intervenes in real life with miracles that only He can perform. He uses people in His plan. Be encouraged to believe God again for yourself, your family and nation.

May He show himself strong on your behalf, give you the desire of your heart and inspire you to take a leap of faith.

His love and mine,
Deborah Starczewski

CHAPTER 1

ADVERSITY, ATTACKS
AND STANDING

In 2001, September 11 took place in New York as I watched the two planes hit the Twin Towers. Then, there were attacks in Washington and the countryside of Pennsylvania where the passengers chose to stand up in the face of adversity. I find it interesting that Revelation 9:11 talks about the destroyer as well. The date is significant and 911 will come in life for us as individuals, too. There are times of emergency and attacks; we all have seasons in life, whether we like it or not.

With the two open-heart surgeries and two mini-strokes that Dan experienced, we had our own 911 attacks. We chose to believe God and put all our hope in Him. In the day in which we live, you would do well to do the same. We are all players with a specific role in the drama of life going on all around us, whether it is personal or corporate. We must each choose to stand in the face of adversity, believe God and learn to trust Him.

We must choose to keep our *shoes of peace* on and believe God, no matter what season we find ourselves in. What Jesus did on the cross for all mankind gives us authority and victory when we choose to stand on the Word of God and do it. We must choose to believe, keep our hope in Christ, stay eternity-minded and stand in the gap through prayer.

We stand in the gap through intercession. Intercession is the act of going on behalf of someone else that needs help from God. It can be prayer for people who have urgent situations that need immediate attention from God. Intercession touches the very heart of God. An intercessor is sensitive to God at all times and totally surrendered to Him. Intercession requires you to become selfless while putting the needs and concerns of others above your own. We are moved by the Spirit of God to pray until peace comes.

I recently watched a great movie named *The Christmas Blessing* on the Hallmark Channel. I observed how God used a pair of red shoes to connect the lives of several families to bring about good. God constantly reminds us of our covering through the blood of Jesus and the authority we have been given as we abide in His Word.

I also remember *The Wizard of Oz* very well and especially the part where Dorothy stands with her ruby red shoes saying: "There is no place like home." We live in this world, but our real home will be forever settled in eternity based on people we choose to follow. Associations have the power to build us up or destroy us. Jesus is our best teacher; He is the only way to heaven and the One we must *choose* to follow. He is our ONLY hope!

YOUR ROLE

The part you hold in life largely depends on your level of intentionality and your understanding of purpose. Life is also determined and altered by **whom we follow** and our level of **obedience** to get to the other side, as well as our **fortitude** and **integrity** with which we do it. Blessing is always on the other side of obedience. God gave Dan his own resurrection story and divinely intervened time and time again. God exposed the enemy at every turn.

"The thief does not come except to steal, and to kill, and

to destroy. I have come that they may have life, and that they may have *it* more abundantly" (John 10:10 NKJV).

Do you suppose God raised Dan up from early death because He knew I didn't want to be a widow at such an early age in life? Do you suppose it had anything to do with the Mercy Seat or the dream God gave me about it at all? Yes! Do you suppose it had anything to do with being a witness and having a huge testimony of God's unfailing love and mercy? The answer is a resounding yes. People need hope again!

God heard our prayers and the cries of our hearts. He still does! He cares deeply and is seated in Heaven. Jesus is seated at the right hand of the Father, praying that our faith will not fail.

There is a fountain that flows from the Mercy Seat. What about the sculpture named the Mercy Seat at Mercy Hospital? That was not a coincidence! The world calls confirmations "coincidences" but there is really no such thing as a coincidence. Life is like a tapestry, brilliantly knitted together by God and you can only see the details if you choose to turn aside to look. What an amazing confirmation in the natural of what God had shown me in a dream. God opened my eyes to see His hand in every detail.

There is power in the Blood of Jesus and He is concerned about your heart. When I crossed over the *threshold* at Mercy Hospital each day I saw the beautiful piece of artwork, which I later learned was named *The Mercy Seat*. God was opening my eyes, yet again, to a new level of revelation—or a leap of faith to believe God in the most adverse circumstances.

THRESHOLD EXPERIENCES

Liminality is a term used to describe a threshold experience. It is from the Latin word *limen*, meaning "a threshold." In Anthropology (the science of "humanity"), liminality is the quality of ambiguity or disorientation that occurs in the middle stage of rituals, when participants no longer hold their pre-ritual status but have not yet begun the transition to the status they will hold when the ritual is complete. During a ritual's liminal stage, participants "stand at the threshold" between their previous way of structuring their identity, time, or community, and a new way, which the ritual establishes.

Merrian-Webster gives the meaning: of or relating to a sensory threshold, barely perceptible, and relating to, or being an intermediate state, phase, or condition: in-between, transition: in the liminal state between life and death. It is composed of danger, marginality, disorientation, or an ordeal and tends to create a space that is neither here nor there, a transitional stage in this drama of life between what was and what is to come.

We are all in a state of transition in life. Transition means movement, passage, or change from one position, state, stage, subject, concept, etc., to another; change: *the transition from adolescence to adulthood*. It can also mean a brief modulation, a passing from one key to another in music, or a sudden unprepared modulation. The word can also mean a passage from one scene to another by sound effects, music, etc., as in a television program, theatrical production, or the like.

A ritual is a set of actions, performed mainly for their symbolic value. It may be prescribed by the traditions of a community, including religious community. The term usually refers to actions that are stylized, excluding actions that are arbitrarily chosen by the performers.

The performers in this drama were many, but the main characters are my husband Daniel and His Lord Jesus. Yes, my husband went into heart failure when they started a heart catheterization and the doctor used the paddles to bring him back to life through the power of God. He was at a place between life and death. Yes, God uses people in his plan for the saving of lives.

WHAT DAN HEARD ON THE O.R. TABLE

Dan actually told me he heard a doctor say, "His vein is twisted." He heard a nurse say vitals were dropping, then another said the same thing—and the doctor said he was pulling out. The procedure was stopped and that is the last thing Dan remembered hearing till the doctor told him they were getting him a room and he was being admitted. You can see clearly that we can hear in transition.

It is the resurrection power of God that empowered Dan to live again. God used the medical staff as part of the healing process. Yes, God uses people and he allows pain to reveal a problem to push us into the purpose for which we are created. God's Word tells me He turns everything out for our good and His glory.

"And we know that in all things God works for the good of those who love him, who have been called according to his purpose" Romans 8:28 (NIV 1984).

Many of the hospital staff told us they had never seen such divine intervention. From one episode to the next, God divinely intervened in Dan's life to bring him back to health and extend his life. I told him he had a new lease on life.

It was kind of strange. He had told me he wanted to go into full-time ministry with me and the next thing we knew, he was in the hospital for twenty-five days sharing about the love of God flat on his back. What a testimony!

(Yes, My Husband Went Into Heart Failure and God Gave Us Our Own Resurrection Story, Healing of the Heart—what a GIFT from God.)

CHAPTER 2

THE WALK IN MERCY

Here I was again—at the Mercy Seat, walking by it daily! The Lord drew my attention to this beautiful rock and tree that was the first thing I saw as I entered over the threshold at Mercy Hospital. It is The ART of MERCY by the artist and craftsman Michael Sherrill and named the "Mercy Seat."

God was giving me a natural manifestation of the dream He had given me. He was showing me how He brings miracles from heaven to earth when we choose to hear and obey Him at the slightest whisper. God goes to extreme measures for the saving of lives spiritually, physically, emotionally and financially. He wants us to put our hope and trust in Him.

As I walked down the long hall to the room where my husband was being prepared for his TEE (Trans-esophageal Echocardiogram), the Holy Spirit said to me, "The son has gone before you"—I realized my husband was in the exact same room our son was in seven years earlier when he was having a heart catheterization to prepare him for open-heart surgery.

A TEE is an alternative way to perform an echocardiogram and gives a better view of the heart. A specialized probe containing an ultrasound transducer at its tip is passed into the patient's esophagus. This allows image and Doppler evaluation that can be recorded and gives clear images of the heart for better diagnosis. Transthoracic ultrasound must traverse skin, fat, ribs and lungs before obtaining reflection of heart back to the probe. (Wikipedia).

A heart catheterization is a procedure with anesthesia where a puncture is made either in the femoral artery in the groin area or in the wrist, if necessary, to insert a plastic sheath with wire inside that is used for numerous procedures and to view inside of heart. (Wikipedia)

Fear tried to grip my heart, but the words of the Lord were far greater than any fear or doubt the enemy would send my way. The love of God was being made evident at every turn. He was preparing me to trust Him in even greater measure.

There are three important men in my life, my father, husband, and son. The other three are God, Jesus and the Holy Spirit that are *most* important—God is my heavenly Father, Jesus is my Savior and Lord, and the Holy Spirit is my helper!

THE WALK WITH OUR SON

Just seven years earlier, we had walked down this same hall in Mercy Hospital with our son prior to his surgery for aortic valve replacement. I will never forget the night I received *his* phone call. I was driving to a church outside of Winston in Clemmons and I just didn't feel well for some reason. I remember telling the Lord I wanted to go home because I had a check in my spirit. I sensed an extreme urgency about something and *then* the call came. My son told me he was running on the treadmill and collapsed. I immediately told him to go to the emergency room across the street at Presbyterian Hospital.

Dan and I drove over to the emergency room as soon as I made it back from Winston to be with our son, Landon, during the waiting process for tests. Yes, life is full of waiting. Waiting is a huge part of life so we may as well get used to it and learn patience. Have you not figured out that life is full of times of waiting yourself?

Landon was released after midnight but advised to see his regular doctor. I kept hearing the Lord saying the word *"bicuspid"* to me. I mentioned it to Dan and he said that it was just a tooth. I knew God was saying something to me concerning Landon but didn't fully understand to start with what it was and I knew it didn't have anything to do with a tooth.

The next day, our son went to see his local doctor who advised him to see a cardiologist. It turned out that he did not have walking pneumonia like the doctors had thought, but instead his aortic valve was *bicuspid* at birth and needed replacing. There was that word!

(A biscuspid aortic valve is an aortic valve that has only two leaflets instead of three. It regulates blow flow from the heart to the aorta, the major vessel that brings blood flow to the body).

It was quite interesting and intense as the Lord prepared Landon for what he had to walk through and prepared us to walk beside him. God was warning us and showing us that He was walking with us each step of the way. **One word from God can bring great change, give you confirmation and ultimately give you hope!**

ANOTHER WORD FROM GOD

The Lord starting speaking the word *"onyx"* to me through a teaching I was listening to while driving the car on how God puts the *onyx* stone in the shoulder of the priests. Then I came home and turned the television on to watch the news—which I don't always do as a routine.

Interestingly enough, I began to watch as they were talking about a million dollar bathroom made out of solid *onyx* and it was white. I always thought onyx was black. We learn something new each day, right? I kept hearing the word *onyx* everywhere I went.

Landon's cardiologist confirmed his problems and sent him to a surgeon who began to share the options for replacement. One of the options was an On-x valve that had just been introduced a couple weeks earlier from a foreign nation. Yes, there was that word; it was just spelled differently. I sensed the Lord was telling me His divine selection but Landon wanted to choose a different option. Imagine that!

Divine guidance comes from the Lord. He cares intimately about every detail in our lives. Pay close attention and you will SEE!

I remember coming home and praying to the Lord, "If this is *Your* choice, please speak to Landon and move on his heart." I didn't want to influence our son with opinions but did tell him how God had been speaking to me with the word onyx, as well as bicuspid.

Not ten minutes after I prayed that prayer, Landon phoned to ask me how to spell onyx. I told him the spelling of the valve was On-x but was like the stone onyx in sound. He ended up choosing that option, as you might of guessed. Needless to say, God supernaturally walked through that season in Landon's life with us and he is still alive today and well with his wife and two children.

God always has a plan—and it is good! He has a great plan for you too! The Bible tells us:

"For I know the plans I have for you, declares the Lord, plans to prosper you and not to harm you, plans to give you hope and a future" (Jer. 29:11 NIV).

INCREDIBLE HULK

To this day, I can still remember seeing Landon in intensive care after the surgery for the first time. He was extremely swollen and in much pain. He looked like one of the Avengers, The Hulk, except he wasn't green. When we came in to see him at first, he was not awake but we were at least able to stand beside him till he awoke.

Pastor Bill and I came in first and he shared a few words with us that I will never forget. He told us he heard the Lord speak something very specific to him. I reflected on the day just a week before when I was at a nail salon and heard the Lord say to me, "I will speak to your son the way I speak to you. He will hear my voice." I remembered calling Landon to share this with him. He said, "Mom, that's a little freaky."

Yes, sometimes as a believer, we can have a problem believing. We can also have a problem understanding that God still speaks. That doesn't change the fact that He still does! God hasn't changed. But has the church? Have you? Do you dare to believe? Has religion dampened your faith? Have you lost your first love for God?

The Bible says, "Jesus Christ is the same yesterday, today, and forever" (Hebrews 13:8 NKJV).

LIFE OR DEATH AND CHOICES

As we stood by Landon, there was one other person in the critical unit who had also had open-heart surgery. The woman beside Landon in this critical unit did not make it. One died and one lived. That is life, my friends.

The one thief heard the words of Jesus on the cross, believed and received Him at the wire just before physical death. The other thief heard but did not believe. That is life today as well. We either believe or we don't. We are either for Jesus or we are against Him. *It is a matter of the heart. God is the great heart surgeon and we must make a choice!*

Even when families have issues, and they will, only God can mend broken hearts, heal hearts, and do surgery when necessary. He is the Great Physician and our healer. I knew my husband needed healing with that cough he had for almost a year. It was so bad that I was hardly able to sleep at night myself. I remember on numerous occasions asking Dan to please go to the doctor and have it checked out, but he simply would not go.

Looking back now, I am not really sure why he wouldn't go but that is not the point. Men can be stubborn. Even his heart surgeon said the same thing.

Here we were again with a potential life and death situation. My father went home to be with the Lord in 2010, our son had heart surgery several years earlier, and here we were again, at another valley to walk through with the Lord by our side.

HEART CHECK

If you are a man reading this and feel anger now because it may seem as though I am generalizing, perhaps God is speaking to your heart to soften it. Ask yourself if you have a stubborn spot in your heart. Women can have stubborn spots too!

Scripture: God will take out the stony, stubborn heart and give you a tender and responsive heart instead. See Ezekiel 36:26.

CHAPTER 3

PRAYER WORKS – How God Revealed the Hidden Truth

Dan had this horrendous cough that seemed to get worse with each passing day. It seemed he had been coughing for nearly a year. Mother agreed as well. Dan was ignoring it or either in denial. I am not sure which.

I simply got so aggravated with him one morning that I told the Lord I had actually had it trying to convince my husband to go the doctor. I remember saying in prayer, "Lord, please speak to Dan yourself as it is obvious he is not listening to me. I am getting really aggravated with him and actually getting angry with you wondering why you won't speak to him yourself. Please send laborers across his path because I don't want to be a widow."

Now I know some of you are wondering why on earth would I say I was getting angry with God about this situation, right? I didn't understand why God wasn't speaking to Dan or could it be that Dan just wasn't listening? I simply did not understand how anyone with such a hacking cough would not realize there was a huge problem. At night, I would wake up and see Dan in this open vision as if he were dead in the bed, just lying there like a pale corpse. *I knew we had a serious problem.*

I did not tell my husband of the visions God was giving me because I didn't want to instill fear in him. I simply knew

God was letting me know the serious nature of this problem for me to pray. I prayed that morning specifically and gave it to God.

Less than two hours later, my husband called to ask me if I would call the doctor and make him an appointment. He said the most interesting thing happened. He informed me he had five clients tell him he needed to get his cough checked over the last couple hours. Imagine that? Wow! You think? God answered immediately and Dan heard and listened!

Yes, Dan told me he was amazed at all the different people telling him to get the cough checked out. Needless to say, I couldn't resist telling him I knew why. I told him what I had prayed and then called to get him an appointment with a local doctor. He went to see her in the late afternoon and she told him she thought it was pertussis or whooping cough.

GOD STILL SPEAKS AND INTERVENES

I recently watched a movie and heard a young lady say she had her heart broken one time this month already. She wasn't sure she could have her heart broken twice in the same month and it not actually be broken for good. I can assure you a heart can have two problems in a month. My husband had two open-heart surgeries; one on February 29th and the next on March 13th. That is two problems, my friends. Pay attention as you read and see how vitally important it is for us to pray and get to know God so we can hear Him.

The Lord gave me another dream to warn me. The next morning I woke up and remembered the dream the Lord had given me in the middle of the night. I saw myself in this clear four sided plexi-glass machine. There was a stream of beautifully colored light purple liquid, like a fountain flowing from myself, through the clouds with the sun shining through, all the way to the **Mercy Seat** in heaven. **(Remember that word as you continue to read!)**

I had a sense of urgency in my spirit but was not worried or upset. A week went by and Dan was not better after taking the prescribed medicines. Dan's doctor had told him if he wasn't better in a week to call back to her office. After we called back, she ordered a chest x-ray for that afternoon and suggested he see a pulmonary specialist.

He had pleural effusions that showed up and I didn't have peace about this at all. I knew something was seriously wrong and no one was listening to me, especially my husband. I wanted them to get moving with the solution!

(Pleural effusions is excess fluid that accumulates between the two pleural layers, the fluid-filled space that surrounds the lungs. Excessive amounts of such fluid can impair breathing. Fluid was accumulating in Dan's lung due to his heart issue.)

The lady on the phone at the front desk at his doctor's office said they would either make the appointment or I could. Since I knew he had a serious problem from the Lord's warnings, I chose to make the calls myself. I was on the phone for over four and a half hours trying to find a specialist that could see him right away. The other places were booked for nearly thirty days.

Finally, I found one in Charlotte that could see him the next day. They told us to be there thirty minutes before the actual appointment with the doctor for testing. He was scheduled to have some type of breathing test before actually seeing the specialist.

The next morning, I could tell Dan was struggling with even walking up the stairs in our home before we left. I can still see the look on his face and hear him gasping for breath. On our drive into the city, we listened to a Christian radio station and I had my prayer book with me praying.

We made it to the parking deck and walked into the specialist's office where we signed in at the front desk. We sat down in the waiting room and some time later his name was called for the breathing test. There is the waiting again. Do you feel like you are always in a waiting room?

We both stood up and walked down the hall to find that four sided plexi-glass like machine just like the one in my dream. I knew we were in trouble but that God was divinely guiding us along. God was giving me signs showing His guidance and peace to go along with it as well.

God still speaks and He divinely intervenes. He tells us in His Word that the Holy Spirit reveals all hidden truth and shows us things to come. Study John chapters 14 through 16 and find out for yourself. This will help you grow and learn to trust God for yourself in greater measure.

After the breathing test, Dan saw the pulmonary specialist. While he was examining my husband, he asked Dan if he knew he had a loud heart murmur. Of course Dan did not know it and the doctor said these words, "We can either move quickly or we can wait three weeks and see how you do with new medicines." I spoke up rather quickly and said we were not waiting any longer and began to explain how long this had actually been going on in the first place. It was not wisdom to be passive any longer. We had to be aggressive.

If God had not warned me through the dreams and visions, I might have trusted the doctor and waited again. Thank God that He still speaks and warns us of things to come so we will move and not wait. There are times to wait and times to act!

The doctor advised Dan he needed a couple more tests and an echocardiogram. (An echocardiogram is a test that uses sound waves to create a moving picture of the heart). He informed us he would have his staff set it up on our way out. We stood in line for a bit and were asked to sit in the waiting room while they worked on scheduling. After a few minutes, one of the staff told us they would call us with the appointments later in the afternoon.

On our way out to the parking garage, Dan was gasping for air again while we walked and talked. We stopped at the soda machines to get him a Diet Pepsi. While we continued to walk, his gasping for air got far worse. I asked him about it but he told me it was the soda. I knew it was not the soda nor was it walking and drinking a soda at the same time that was causing him to gasp for air. Something was seriously wrong! Men!

We finally made it to the car and proceeded to drive. We arrived home and Dan drove onto our office in Winston. After a few hours I called back to the specialist's office to find out the schedule for Dan's tests to learn it would be about a week for one and ten days for the other at Presbyterian Hospital.

As you read my account of the hope that God instills in His children, it is my prayer that God will fill your heart with His love and empower you to believe God for yourself. I pray that God will open your eyes to see His hand at every turn in your life as well. It is my prayer this will be the best day of your life. Eternity is real. You don't know how many more days of life you actually have to live. Keep reading.

I had an extreme sense of urgency and saw for myself the way my husband's health was declining, so I picked up the phone and called Sanger Heart and Vascular to ask if they could work Dan in for an echocardiogram and explained the details of what was happening.

Olivia at the cardiologist's office was extremely nice on the phone but explained they were booked the next day. Not five minutes later, I had a message on my phone from her asking me to call the next morning because they were going to work him in for an appointment. It was five minutes after five when the message game through. Their office was closed so I had to wait. I don't know how I missed that call. The phone didn't even ring and it was now after five o'clock. More waiting. That's what we do most in life, right?

The next morning I called and spoke to the person in charge of scheduling who said they didn't usually schedule the test before the patient would see the cardiologist, but with the problems Dan was having he was going to ask if he could schedule it that way. He called me back shortly with an appointment for the next day, February 22nd.

Thank God for persistence and the Holy Spirit who guides us along our path in life. Dan had the echocardiogram the next day and we were to meet Dr. Bower of Sanger Clinic the following day for results on the 23rd. I will never forget that first meeting.

Dan was not too happy to hear the doctor tell him that his mitral valve was worn out and he had less than a week to live. Dan has an accounting firm with a partner and he wanted to have it done on April 18th, after tax season. My God, help me Lord Jesus. Yes, that is the epitome of a businessman's response at a new height, don't you think? He wanted to wait till *after* tax season. I've got news for you. Newsflash! There are times you better not wait any longer!

All it takes is one storm in life to let us know we are not in control. Needless to say, Dan was not in control of his life situation and God was warning him of things to come. He had a choice to make. Dr. Bower told my husband he wouldn't be alive by next Friday if he didn't have surgery. Dr. Bower was going to schedule a TEE for the next day, Friday, February 24th.

It was a quiet drive home as Dan was not a happy camper with the recent news. He drove onto Winston and I took Mother to lunch at a local restaurant. Interestingly enough, my cell phone rang at lunch and it was Dr. Bower. It had been about one hour and a half since we left his office. I can still hear the sound of his voice and remember him telling me he hoped Dan made the right choice about having surgery rather than waiting till after tax season because he wouldn't live otherwise.

He also wanted to know if I thought Dan would agree to have a heart catheterization the next day after the TEE. I told him I thought he would since he would already be there anyway, but I would ask. He was going to be a captive audience anyway, right? He also encouraged me and said he hoped Dan made a right decision in moving forward quickly as he thought he had less than a week to live.

HEART CHECK

"One day when the crowds were being baptized, Jesus himself was baptized. As he was praying, the heavens opened, and the Holy Spirit descended on him in the form of a dove. And a voice from heaven said, "You are my beloved Son, and I am fully pleased with you" ----Luke 3:21-22 NLT

As Jesus prayed, we learn the windows of heaven opened and the Holy Spirit descended in the form of a dove. When we pray, God releases His Spirit that brings whatever we need at the time. Without prayer, we will never be able to see heaven open—or experience the miraculous power of the Holy Spirit. We see a natural manifestation of what was happening in the Spirit!

Ask yourself this question: Am I praying and seeing the power of God in my life with answered prayer?

CHAPTER 4

WE MUST GET IN AGREEMENT WITH GOD'S PLAN

W hether it is for America, the nations, or our own personal family or even finances, we must choose to get in agreement with God's plan. Have you learned how to do that yet? You do know there is hope in God, right? If you don't know that for sure, please pay close attention as you read this book, for you will realize there is hope again in Jesus and the finished work at Calvary. The blood of Jesus has been sprinkled on the Mercy Seat and He is seated at the right hand of the Father, interceding for you and I that our faith would not fail. God calls us to speak out for innocent lives and for the unborn. He calls us as the church to confront sin and moral decay and to defend the poor and oppressed. He also calls us to pursue peace and bless Israel. Jesus is the King of Kings and Lord of Lords.

He is our only hope! When you are faced with doubt, despair and loss of hope, no matter what your situation, please turn your heart toward the One True God! Jesus is our only hope! It is not your bank account, your next new job or career, or trust in yourself—but in Jesus Christ Himself and the finished work on the cross at Calvary.

I knew my husband, Dan, had to get into agreement with God's plan as his cardiologist gave him the news if he wanted to live. Dr. Bower told him he had less than a week to live with his mitral valve worn out unless he agreed to surgery. He obviously had a genetic problem at work since birth. His grandfather, who was a businessman, died at an early age from probably the same problem unaware.

The Holy Spirit had revealed the problem to me and now had made it evidently clear through Dr. Bower's words to Dan. He had heard the report and was warned he had to move quickly, if he wanted to live. Who was he going to believe? What would he do? I can assure you, Dan was not a happy camper with the news he had just received.

We had two choices. We could listen to Dr. Bower, move quickly and trust God or Dan could wait and die early. Dr. Bower had told me he hoped Dan made the right choice and so did I. I wanted my husband to live. I chose to believe God was at work even in the midst of the life and death situation.

THE SLAB OF HAM AND TESTING

Dinner at the restaurant that evening was quite humorous. Dan rarely eats pork but that night, he ordered a slab of ham. Yes, it covered the entire plate. I looked at Dan's plate and thought to myself, "What on earth is he doing?" Dan very rarely eats pork, so I guess he thought he would just have a slab of ham. It wasn't a small piece. Guess he thought he might as well eat whatever he wanted if he only had a week to live. I told Dan about Dr. Bower's phone call earlier in the day and his conversation with me about having a second test as well. Dan agreed to do both tests! There is always a time of testing in our lives as well!

The next day, our dear friends Rick and Susan met us at Mercy Hospital on Vail Avenue to sit with us in the waiting room. Landon and his wife came over to sit with me and Mother as well. It is good to be surrounded by loving family and friends.

The medical staff took Dan back and advised they would

come and get me shortly so I could speak to him before they did the first procedure. After a time of waiting, they called for me to come and see my husband. As I walked down the long hall to the room where my husband was being prepared for his TEE (Trans-esophageal Echocardiogram), the Holy Spirit said to me, "The son has gone before you"—I realized they had my husband in the exact same room our son was in seven years earlier when he was having a heart catheterization before open-heart surgery. The Lord, in His sweetness, was showing me a natural manifestation of what was actually happening.

The Son of God, Jesus, has already gone before us and everything we have need of was accomplished through His shed blood on the Cross of Calvary. His Blood is on the Mercy Seat and that is where He is seated today to the right of the Father God. That is good news my friends. That is the Good News of the Gospel of Jesus Christ.

God, Himself, was encouraging me. That is the love of God!

RHEMA WORDS

I remember the Lord had spoken a Scripture to my heart... Zechariah 4:1-2 and I knew the Lord was speaking to me that He would show me things to come. He also gave me Amos 3:7 the same day that He gave me the dream about the four sided plexi-glass machine. God also gave me Zech. 6:4. Here are the following verses:

"Then the angel who had been talking with me returned and woke me, as though I had been asleep. "What do you see now?" he asked" (Zechariah 4:1-2 NLT)

"And what are these, my lord?" I asked the angel who was talking with me" (Zechariah 6:4 NLT)

Indeed, the Sovereign Lord never does anything until he reveals his plans to his servants the prophets. (Amos 3:7 NLT)

(A great book to read to help you further understand is *"The Harbinger"* by Jonathan Cahn)

Fear tried to grip my heart, but the words of the Lord were far greater than any fear or doubt the enemy would send my way. A perfect verse to combat fear is 2 Timothy 1:7. The Bible says, "For God has not given us a spirit of fear, but of power, love, and self-discipline (2 Tim. 1:7 NLT). *You begin to say it yourself. Yes, out loud. Don't worry what anyone else thinks.*

The love of God was being made evident to me at every turn. He was preparing me to trust Him in even greater measure. He was also preparing Dan to trust Him in far greater measure and giving him a huge testimony of the goodness of God.

Yes, just seven years earlier, we had walked down this same hall in Mercy Hospital with our son prior to testing for valve replacement. I remember feeling total peace but a sense of intensity and dependency upon the Lord just like I did seven years earlier with Landon. Here we were again...same hospital. You see, now both of the men in my life—my son and my husband were taking a walk in Mercy.

It is essential that we all learn to pray God's Word. Your words carry success, creative force and have the power to activate angels. The Bible says, "Bless the LORD, you His angels, who excel in strength, who do His word, heeding the voice of His word" (Psalm 103:20 NKJV).

Today, while I was editing this book, the Lord gave me an amazing verse. The Bible says, "The LORD will guide you continually, And satisfy your soul in drought, And strengthen your bones; You shall be like a watered garden, And like a spring of water, whose waters do not fail" (Isaiah 58:11 NKJV). Yes, He continually guides me and He wants to guide you.

HEART CHECK

Ask yourself these questions:
Am I being spirit-controlled, motivated, and empowered?
Am I living more in the flesh than in the Spirit?
Am I living more in the flesh than in the Spirit in these areas?

1. Lusts and sexual passions
2. Manipulate others or manipulated by other people
3. Work, career, and ambition
4. Substance abuse or addictions
5. Love of money, materialism, technology, or greed
6. Religious tradition or legalism
7. Pride, position, power
8. Doubts and fears

CHAPTER 5

REFLECTIONS WHILE WE WAITED

MY WALK WITH JESUS AND DADDY

Today as we were driving home from the office where I was editing this book, the Lord had painted the sky with the most beautiful hues of pink and lavender. The reflections of color made the sky look like a beautiful portrait, hand-painted by God Himself.

When you take a walk with someone you love, do you steam ahead like a drill sergeant or do you take time to enjoy the day and actually talk to the person? Do you know how to walk and enjoy where you are at present?

God causes us to reflect at different times in life. Reflect with me as I share what we recently walked through over the course of two years that ended on January 30th, 2010 at 5:17 PM. That was the night the Lord took my daddy home to heaven. The accounts in this chapter flooded my mind as we waited at Mercy with Dan.

On January 30th the grounds at the High Point Cancer Center were covered with freshly fallen snow that was absolutely beautiful. It was like a blanket of clouds had floated down from heaven and had perfectly covered the earth with angels standing all around.

My family had some of our fondest memories with snow covering the earth. We all loved playing in the snow with our family and friends, picking out a Christmas tree and other times that God blessed us with snowflakes that seemed to fall straight from heaven. I can remember praying and asking God to let it snow many times, and it would snow.

While staying in High Point after my dad was admitted to the Cancer Center, I had to drive to Charlotte to take our car to the dealership. That morning a warning light came on indicating a problem. I called the service department to learn it was the Co2 light. That was amazing as Dad was having a problem with Co2 and had a Bi-Pap machine assisting in helping him breathe.

God always gives us a natural manifestation in life to show us what is going on—if we pay attention.

I drove down I-85 and had to take a detour on highway 64 due to roadwork that finally brought me back out to the interstate. I remembered my daddy telling me he had cut trees for that road to be built either before he was in the Armed Services or just after. I began to see that God had used my natural daddy to prepare the way for me to even drive on the freeway that very day.

After I arrived in Charlotte, I stopped at a store to purchase some makeup since I had been at the hospital for over two weeks and needed to buy some. The Lord drew my attention to this teardrop shaped bottle that had different colors of specs with a dark colored base. I picked it up and saw the name of the perfume: MIDNIGHT RAIN.

I began to share the story of what happened with the salesclerk and she was deeply touched by the way God was revealing Himself to me. That is the love of God, my friends! The night before God had given me a dream about rain at midnight and I also felt the Lord was showing me He would have the respiratory therapist who had grown so fond of my daddy called back into work. He was also showing me the perfume bottle called MIDNIGHT RAIN. Only God could orchestrate all the details that He was revealing.

When we cry out to God because we love Him, even when we feel like we are at a midnight hour, God sends spiritual rain to refresh and encourage us. He sends the rain of the Holy Spirit that brings restoration, healing and deliverance. He delivered Paul and Silas this way as they praised and worshiped God in prison.

I chose to call the respiratory therapist and tell her what the Lord had shown me. We had become good friends over the course of my daddy's stay and I had her cell phone number and email. *You can choose to develop relationships with people when you are given an opportunity, even in the midst of adversity.* She was scheduled off for a few days, but I sensed the Lord was showing me He would have the hospital call her to come back to work that day.

She had been a great help and would even bring my daddy nutritional drinks that either she or one of us would feed him. We would have to lift the Bi-Pap machine to give him just a minute of air in between drinking the liquid. (A Bi-Pap machine is used to assist people who have a problem in getting air to their lungs.)

Dad didn't want to smother to death. That was a fear of his and we were not going to allow that to happen on our watch. Early that morning, the hospital called her back to work just as the Lord had revealed. God was positioning her to be with us on my daddy's last day on earth and God used the Bi-Pap machine to let me know we were about to say good-bye to our papa.

MORE REFLECTION

As I continued to drive to Charlotte, I was praying and asking God to make sure I could be with my daddy when he died. I wanted to be by his side. When I arrived at the dealership, to my surprise, the bay area was actually closed. Party trucks, flower trucks and food trucks were parked in front and a beautiful red carpet was laid right up to the white canopies that stopped just where they told me to park my car. It was also a handicapped spot where they directed me to park.

Our service representative, Kevin, met me at the carpet and asked if I was coming to the party. I told him I didn't get an invitation. He assured me I did get one in the mail, but I began to explain God was warning me of the things to come prophetically—that God was planning a party for my daddy to come home to Him. I would not be able to come to that party.

I walked into the bay area with Kevin where I saw beautiful rows of fresh red and white flowers everywhere. My heart sank, but I knew God was showing me what was to come next. I left my white car and they gave me a black loaner car to drive.

I called my husband and he met me in Cornelius where we followed each other to High Point Hospital. I began to think about how God had shown me the party that was being planned. Then I wondered about the time of the party so I called the dealership to inquire. No one answered the phone at the dealership, which I thought was strange. Apparently, God was not going to show me the exact time. I had to trust His timing was going to be perfect.

I remember telling Dan I felt like one of God's favorite kids because of the way He was continually revealing things to me. After we arrived at the parking deck at the hospital, we pulled our cars in and parked side by side. I noticed a car to the left of us with a sign saying: FAVORITE.

Dan and I both smiled! God has a sense of humor, don't you think? He goes to extreme measures to encourage us and to get us to believe Him. I love how He is always at work, even when we might not notice. Then it began to snow.

THE LIGHTS GLISTENING ON THE SNOW

Yes, it began to snow! It seemed as if God covered the earth that day with a beautiful blanket of freshly fallen snow—just for us that day, to take Daddy home! Dad loved snow! As a family, we had some of our fondest memories with the grounds covered with snow that seemed to make the earth still and silent like no other time. It gives you a sense of peace and hope. I can still remember the beauty that day and the view out the window.

It was that field of white lights that the Lord Himself had shown my daddy in an open-vision. He was showing him things to come and giving us time to spend with him before his transition from life here to heaven. It was just like the movie, *FIELD OF DREAMS*.

The last seventeen days of his life, we surrounded him in the Cancer Center and never left his side. I would lay my head on my daddy's chest where I could hear his heart and he would place his hand on my head. My sister would do the same thing. We were Daddy's girls.

Prior to his death, he would ask me when the Lord was coming to take him home. He would say it repeatedly throughout the night. My sister would answer and he would say, "Pamela, go back to sleep. I'm asking your sister" then he would say, "Deborah, Deborah, when is HE coming for me?"

The Lord gave my daddy a dream where he was talking with his sister and her husband. Interestingly enough, they were both in heaven. I asked my dad how long he thought he had spoken to them. I knew the Lord was showing us that our daddy would soon be in heaven too.

I had lost one of the three most important men in my life and here we were again at a crisis point at Mercy with Dan. The incredible way the Lord showed me Daddy was sick and walked with us through that two-year journey was priceless. God never ceases to amaze us with His love even through the hard times.

CHAPTER 6

THE FIELD OF WHITE LIGHTS

I'll never forget hearing my daddy's voice telling me he had a vision of a field of white lights outside the window. Mother said he had a dream but Daddy assured me it was not a dream; it was a vision. He was awake. My heart sank as I thought of the movie "Field of Dreams" and sensed the Lord leading us down a path that would be sad but He would walk with us; and He did just that. The earth was covered with snow and the stars glistening upon it created a field of white lights.

HUNGRY LIVE

I will also never forget the morning the Lord spoke to my heart to look under our bed before I began to stay in High Point with our family. I can assure you there's nothing ever under our bed but in obedience, I got out of bed to take a peak. As I lifted up the comforter, I could see something glistening as the sun shone through the blinds in the window next to our bed. I saw something but wasn't really sure what it was. I reached underneath to pull out an unopened CD. It had a little boy on the cover with blonde hair that could have passed for my daddy when he was a child.

As I was driving to the hospital that day, I chose to listen to this new CD to hear beautiful music. I wasn't paying much attention to the words as my phone kept ringing and I was speaking with different people updating them on Daddy's situation. I arrived at the hospital in just under two hours and walked into the hospital.

As I think back now and reflect upon all that has happened, the three most important men in my life had been in crisis situations with death knocking at the door. One went home to be with the Lord and my son is a miracle to be alive today. Here we were again at a crisis point in need of a miracle and God's divine intervention.

God used the CD (HUNGRY LIVE) to reveal what was happening and what was to come. God also wants us to be *hungry and thirsty for more of Him while we live on earth. As I think about it all now, I can see, as you will, how God began to unveil the pages of this precious life and showed us it was also drawing to a close. This will happen to all of us at some point in time.*

Needless to say, I am a woman who pays attention to detail. When I tried to order more of the same CD, I was informed it never existed or was out of print. It is actually not available anymore. I don't know how it got under the bed, but God does! How it happened doesn't really matter much. The fact is—God used the CD to minister to us. There are so many divine interventions and places you can't deny the hand of God that you should want to know God for yourself in greater measure!

God was confirming the vision my daddy had about the field of white lights through the words on the CD. After I left the hospital that day, I began to listen to the words as I drove. All of a sudden, there were the words of my dad's vision... "Walking the field of white lights" and my heart sank. For a long period of time, on my drive back and forth, I kept listening to the same CD as God used it to minister to me. This period of time consisted of much driving back and forth from our home to Asheboro and then onto High Point.

I kept it in my car the entire time we walked through this season in our lives. We listened to it playing softly in the background on every drive to the hospital for tests and treatments. I drove from our home to Asheboro to pick them up and take them to the hospital. We made a day of it and would have lunch when Daddy felt like it. I chose to enjoy each day and valued every moment with my parents during this season. You can choose to enjoy time spent with people, no matter what is going on around you too. I chose to abide in my daddy's presence.

THE VIEW FROM THE GLASS WINDOW

Dan and I were returning home from Seoul, Korea where we had been at a Leadership Growth Conference for people in ministry. Our suitcases were packed and I had one thing that reminded me of my daddy. It was a *snow globe with a Father and a young blonde girl on his knee*—it broke in flight on the trip home.

Somehow, I knew something was wrong with my daddy and I would soon learn what I knew in my heart was true. Sometimes we have to learn to believe what is in our heart before we can see it with our eyes.

The glass that encased the window of the snow globe was broken—shattered and my husband threw it away. All of the snow and liquid had come out when it broke. Snow globes are one of my favorite keepsakes as they hold fond memories of us in the snow and our favorite time of the year—Christmas. My daddy loved snow globes too!

Nobody knows when life will end through death *or rapture*. God knows all the details and desires that all come to know Him. This is why is it imperative to have an eternal view of life. You don't really know what night will be your last on earth.

The last night I spent with both parents alive in our home place was quite interesting as well. I didn't sleep much because I would get up to check on my daddy's health. I would walk down the hall just to see his little head sticking up above his favorite recliner. I would carefully listen for his breathing, as not to wake him up, so he could get some rest. He was uncomfortable sleeping in the bed while lying down, so he would sit in his favorite chair. Sometimes he would sleep and sometimes he would read his Bible.

The next morning, I was coming into the family room and saw my daddy fall on the front porch through the *front window*. The view I saw of my daddy through the glass window was disheartening. His legs were simply giving out from weakness and GBS—Guillian Barre' Syndrome. He also had a form of lung cancer. (Guillian-Barre Syndrome is a serious disorder that occurs when the body's defense (immune) system mistakenly attacks part of the nervous system. This leads to nerve inflammation that causes muscle weakness and can damage the myelin sheath (the nerve's covering) causing acute inflammatory demyelinating poly-neuropathy. If often follows a minor infection, sometimes brought about after an adverse reaction to a flu shot, lung infection or gastrointestinal infection. I learned if anyone in your family has ever had Guillian-Barre it is recommended that you never get a flu shot. GBS can also bring about severe muscle weakness to paralysis.)

That was the last day he spent at home. The picture I saw the day he fell on the front porch, as I was standing in the living room, is forever etched in my mind. I quickly called the ambulance to come and when they arrived to take him back to the hospital, Mother and I followed in our car. I called my sister at work and she met us at the hospital.

I remembered my conversation with Daddy the night before about death. He told me he didn't want to die, but if it was his time and the *train* was coming for him, he said he was ready to go. I paid careful attention to his words.

We followed behind the ambulance and came to the

railroad tracks where for the first time we had to wait for an oncoming *train* to pass. I knew the Lord was revealing to me why my daddy talked about the train. We had been driving on that same road for nearly two years without ever being stopped by a passing train on the trips to the hospital. He lived another seventeen days as you can read in my timeline of events.

For the first time ever, the Lord allowed me to hear the first line of the song I had been listening to for months. It said, "Coming up to the place I die…" and I knew God was allowing us to be stopped by the train to reveal His plan that Dad was about to die. My daddy's words rang true in my ears. He passed away in January and went home to be with the Lord. He transitioned from earth to be with His Lord in heaven for all eternity.

There is so much more, I am going to write a book about it too. Stay tuned for that one in more detail. That was my daddy's walk with God and His great mercy that never fails. This all seemed to flash across my mind while I was waiting on Dan. It was like a movie that was replaying across my mind as I sat and waited in the order that God brought it.

CHAPTER 7

THE VIEW FROM THE WINDOW AT MERCY

After reflecting on the loss of my daddy, I realized here I was again—at another life and death challenge with my husband—another valley with a different view of snow. As we sat in the waiting room, the windows were laced with beautiful hand-cut snowflakes that were carefully displayed on each windowpane. There was no freshly fallen snow outside, but God was getting my attention.

God gives each of us windows of time—windows which we can choose to see through and grasp the details. These windows hold pictures of hope for all who choose to turn aside and behold.

We had a window of *hope in God*, as Dan was much younger than my daddy. The view out this window did not have freshly fallen snow, but God was still getting my attention. God has trained me to pay attention to details. This is one of the ways the Holy Spirit speaks to us.

Thoughts and memories of periods of time can flood your mind as you sit quietly and wait. God had allowed all this to pass through the corridors of my mind like a beautiful canvas of His divine handprint for me to reflect upon while I waited. This was hope He was giving me to trust Him, yet again. God took my daddy home, but our son made it through his open-heart surgery.

Here we were again—taking the same walk with my husband. I walked into the same room where our son had been years earlier to sit down with Dan. The nurse warned me about an object sticking out of the wall so I would be careful not to lean back and hit my head. I sat in the chair in an awkward position as they prepped Dan for the procedure. She was a delightful nurse and made me feel extremely welcome and comfortable. I waited with my husband as she began to prep him for the procedure.

I kissed Dan and we always say those three words, "I love you" before I walked back down the hall to the waiting room. After time had passed, the nurses called me back where I met another cardiologist who actually did the procedure, not Dr. Bower. The physicians at Sanger are all exceptional.

I knew this cardiologist from Landon's visits after his surgery. He looked at me, placed his arm on my shoulder and told me Dan was going to be fine. He informed me the staff had failed to schedule Dan for a heart catheterization and he felt he would be fine to have it done on Monday.

Even though the doctor tried to give me assurance that Dan would be fine, I did not have peace because the only person we are to hope in is Jesus. I thank God that He has trained me to hear Him and trust His voice above all else and *not people or opinions, no matter their title*. The name of JESUS is above all and what the Holy Spirit speaks to us is always right.

This is why it is vital to have a personal relationship with the Holy Spirit and spend time in the Lord's presence—so you recognize His voice and can obey His instructions. Always operate in peace. Let peace be your umpire.

I did not have peace at all so I walked back down the hall to the waiting room and called Sanger. I asked to speak to the scheduler and they sent their manager over to speak with me in the waiting room. I shared my concerns and the fact that it wasn't our fault there was a scheduling problem.

I asked them to please call their on-call surgeon in to do the heart catheterization.

I remember talking to Pastor Rick about it and telling him I didn't have peace about waiting. He agreed with me as well. The manager at Sanger was very understanding and agreed to set it up.

We waited again as the hospital staff took Dan to another operating room for the procedure. We waited again! I guess you've figured out by now that what we do most in life is wait, right?

Time passed again and then I heard my name being called and stood up to speak with the physician. I walked out into the hall where he informed me Dan had gone into heart failure and he had to use the paddles to raise him up. They were not even able to finish the heart catheterization. They were admitting him to CCU through the weekend to get him stable enough for surgery.

Thank God the Holy Spirit reveals all hidden truth and shows us things to come. He had warned me through a sense of urgency not to wait. If I had waited and not obeyed, Dan would have gone into heart failure in the car on the drive home. Always trust the Holy Spirit and His promptings and put your faith and hope in God, not people. Don't go against peace in your own heart.

Pay attention to the promptings of the Holy Spirit. When in doubt, seek counsel. For wisdom is found in counsel. Pastor Rick didn't agree on waiting either. Thank God He had someone positioned with us that agreed we should not wait till Monday. God always has what you need nearby if you are paying attention.

Dan was moved to the critical unit where we waited with him again. We prayed for God to stabilize Dan's body for surgery and for him to live! We prayed Psalm 118:17 over him constantly.

We prayed: "He will live and not die, and declare all

the miracles of God"—my translation.

This was a great day. God's resurrection power was manifested in Dan's life.

What is your best day ever? I am so thankful for every minute God has allowed me to remember in this twenty-five day period. I remember knocking the baseball out of the park into the field at a game. Yes, I did that! I remember the fun in the snow on sleds. I remember the good times and the hard moments we all have to face in life.

Take a leap of faith and please believe! I remember the look in the surgeon's face, his words, and the place we were standing in Mercy when he told me what happened to my husband. There are some days we will never forget.

I am forever grateful to God for resurrection day that still empowers us to live again. God sent His resurrection power into Dan and gave him life again.

I have shared details of events in different phases of my life and those that I love, not to confuse you, but to give you examples of the amazing God that loves us and cares about the details in the life of His children. It is my heart's desire that you dare to believe again and have hope in God!

At some point, you will have to choose to cross over and believe, or not!

CHAPTER 8

THE CROSSOVER
AT PROVIDENCE

I remember the nurses telling me I needed to take care of things before the surgery so if there were errands I needed to handle, now would be the time. After surgery things would be more intense, so I decided to get a few things done before Sunday.

I left the hospital to do some errands and remember feeling a slight moment of panic just as I got in my car about to leave. I heard the Lord just as clear as I would be speaking with my own husband say to me, "What do you do?" I answered, "I commit Dan to You Lord, because you promise to take care of all that concerns me" and I pulled out of the hospital parking lot and went straight over on Colonial Avenue up to the next stop sign.

Wow! Someone had placed a sticker underneath the word *STOP*. *Here is what I saw, "STOP WORRYING."* Only God could arrange that one. Someone had put a sticker with the word "worrying" just below the word "stop" on the sign. Can you imagine that? God was, yet again, making sure I knew He had gone before me to make every crooked place straight and to keep my hope in Him. The Holy Spirit was comforting me at every turn and now at a stop sign. That is the love of God, my friends. This may seem small to you, but the smallest detail of encouragement is HUGE in God. He speaks to us at every turn *if* we are listening and watching!

I felt peace to leave and went to a couple appointments. On one of the appointments, I actually met a lady who was also a physician and knew the heart surgeon. God used her words to give me great encouragement as well. I could see God positioning people in my path to reassure me of His presence and His plan. What are the odds of running an errand and meeting a nurse who starts talking about the heart surgeon we were just about to have perform Dan's surgery? That is God! She told me Dan's surgeon had been trained as a pediatric heart surgeon. I knew he would obviously pay great attention to detail and dealing with a child's heart is probably more intense.

God wants us to have the heart of child and believe in childlike faith—even in the most adverse circumstances. God never ceases to amaze me with His divine intervention and His attention to detail. He clearly sets our days in such a way that we know it is totally God and can only be Him. All of this happened at a nail salon in Charlotte. God can speak and reveal Himself in normal, everyday life.

On my drive back, just as I crossed over Providence Road, my heart felt like it was doing flip flops and I sensed something was very wrong. I happened to be on the phone talking with Melanie Campbell and I told her what I was feeling. We began to pray!

I began to pray scriptures and what I sensed the Lord placing in my heart to say. I remember thanking the Lord we were *on His mind* and I heard Him clearly say, "You are not on my mind, you are in my mind." I looked ahead and saw a sign on the back of a car...IN MY MIND. Now, I am here to tell you that only God could divinely arrange all of this. These were clear signs that only the God of the Universe could orchestrate just for my encouragement... simply because He loves us as His children. He was making sure I knew He was paying great attention to every detail.

Melanie and I were both moved by the love of God and how He was going out of His way to show Himself strong on our behalf during this critical time. I parked the car and just as I walked over the threshold at Mercy Hospital I realized my heart felt normal again. I noticed a beautiful rock and tree to my right as I came through the front entrance. It was a beautiful sculpture. I had noticed it before but someone was always sitting on it as I passed by.

I got into the elevator and made it back to CCU where I saw the look on the sweet nurse's face. She began to explain that Dan's heart had gone into a-fib but had gone back into normal rhythm just a few minutes before I showed back up. I remember thinking to myself "Dan's heart went into a-fib and you are a fibber for not calling me" and I gently told her to keep the air light in such an intense time as you can imagine.

What I did realize was that God was allowing me to feel in my heart what was happening in Dan's heart in CCU while I was away. Because He and I are one, I could feel what my husband was feeling. God was assuring me on every turn. I can remember waking up the night I went home at 2:30 AM in the morning with an excruciating headache. Since I was awake, I called the nurses' station to inquire about Dan. The nurse that answered the phone told me he had just given Dan something for a terrible headache. You see, God was showing me what was happening with my husband, yet again.

This same day, God gave me several scriptures: Psalm 71:19-24, Psalm 72:1-7 so I began to read and pray them.

"Your righteousness, O God, reaches to the highest heavens. You have done such wonderful things. Who can compare with you, O God? You have allowed me to suffer much hardship, but you will restore me to life again and lift me up from the depths of the earth. You will restore me to even greater honor and comfort me once again" (Psalm 71:19-24 NLT)

I had prayed to God to save Dan from death and He gave me a funny scripture. He spoke to my heart to specifically read Psalm 71:18. After reading the verse, I told the Lord, "Dan isn't really old yet, but he does have gray hair."

"Now that I am old and gray, do not abandon me, O God. Let me proclaim your power to this new generation, your mighty miracles to all who come after me" (Psalm 71:18 NLT).

God gave me His answer! He gave us a word to stand on, to hope and believe for life!

I kept encouraging myself and others by telling them, "Just like the life of Joseph, God was positioning us, yet again, for full-time ministry." We had our intercessory prayer team praying for Dan and I would give them daily updates. Jewell, who heads it up, said that several people were saying they needed to come and sit with me but she said this to them, "Deborah will be talking to everyone at Mercy. Revival will break out. She doesn't need anyone to entertain. She is about The Father's business."

We also had many pastors and ministries praying from America to India. God places people in your life on purpose. Dare to connect with others and *believe God* to hope again! Don't give up in the waiting! God had Dan working full-time from the hospital bed—he was working on hearts while God worked on his.

I would sit in the chair and write on my Blackberry phone in the dark. Melanie told me that the stars shine brightest on the darkest nights. Yes, we had some intense nights at Mercy, but I have to say, I was never in the dark. My Father did not allow me to sink into despair at any turn. He kept us aware of His divine presence and ministered to us Himself. He is able to use us, even in adversity, when our trust is in Him.

HEART CHECK:

Ask yourself these questions:

Am I focused on eternity or am I too caught up in circumstances?

Is God able to use me when I am faced with adversity or find myself in a tough place?

Do I really trust God with my life, family and circumstances?

"Cast your cares on the LORD and he will sustain you; he will never let the righteous fall" (Psalm 55:22 NIV 1984).

CHAPTER 9

GOD'S PLAN FOR SURGERY – LEAP YEAR DAY

We sat beside Dan and watched the machines to see how his heart and body were responding. I could not sleep and I sat up all night on a chair watching the machines. Mother tried to sleep in the other chair in the room as well.

When I did start to doze off, the machine would wake me up. Then the bed would make a noise like a jet taking off because it had an air compressor to raise the bed up and down. God was keeping us up to watch. God calls us the "Watchmen" on the wall. We are called to "watch and pray."

I am well aware the doctors probably wanted us to go home—but the Lord had clearly spoken to me to stay. He is our advocate and he places us in the lives of others to be theirs as well. My place was beside my husband.

Several different medical staff came in to meet and talk with us prior to scheduling surgery after the display of God's divine intervention. Dan's cardiovascular surgeon came in to meet with us and I knew I liked his last name—Watts. His name represented power to me! Dr. Bower recommended him so I knew he had to be a great surgeon. *Trust me, I was taking every word of encouragement God was sending to me.*

I did ask the Lord to confirm it to me as I had listened to family telling me I should move him to Winston or Raleigh/Durham area hospitals. I felt like a twenty-four hour counselor as I explained to them we were not vacillating in our decision and were not moving. It never ceases to amaze me that people reason and try to tell everyone else what to do. Not much has changed since what happened in the Garden of Eden with Adam and Eve.

I kept receiving texts advising me to move Dan to another hospital. Dan said we were not listening to anyone else and it was our decision. People are double-minded, operate in the flesh with extremes in their emotions; and are not so good at running their own lives, much less ours. Jesus compares people to sheep. I have heard that sheep are the dumbest animals. Does that surprise you? I don't really know if that is true, or not. I do know sheep need a shepherd.

I knew we were right where we were supposed to be because God works *all things out for our good and His glory.* (See Romans 8:28) We simply believed God at His very word! I listened to numerous conversations giving me their insight and their recommendations to the point of exhaustion. I knew the enemy was attacking their minds with reasoning so I simply told them we were exactly where God ordained us to be for the saving of Dan's life and we were trusting God.

This went on for hours. As a matter of fact, if I had listened to them and had Dan moved at all, he would have died on the transfer because as it was, he went into heart failure during the heart catheterization procedure. If we had not been persistent in having the heart catheterization that Dr. Bower had actually ordered and waited till Monday, Dan would have died in the car on the way home after the TEE. Thank GOD for the Holy Spirit prompting me and for the staff at Sanger who heard my heart to move ahead to do it that same day.

God divinely intervened at every turn to save my husband's life and I am forever grateful to God and the staff He used at Mercy Hospital on Vail Avenue. The heart facility has now been moved to Pineville. What a great hospital—CMC MERCY on Vail Avenue. It was like God removed a veil from our natural eyes and opened them to see His hand at work in the most amazing ways! What a God!

WATCHING AND WAITING

We stayed in Critical Care all weekend watching and waiting for Dan's heart to become stable enough for surgery. The Lord informed me the surgery would be on 2/29/2012 and it would be like it never happened. I thought, "Well that's great...that is leap year day." It would surely be a leap of faith as well.

I am thankful that God did not fully share all the details with me for what was to come.

The surgeon came in to tell us he had scheduled surgery for 2/28 and then later changed it to March 1st. I had shared what the Lord spoke to my heart with Dan and a few close people about 2/29 and what God had said about Leap Year Day.

The next day, again the heart surgeon came in and talked with us about having to change his surgery to 2/29 for logistical reasons to get the right team in place. You do know that the right team is important, don't you? I knew this was God's plan all along because He makes sure every crooked place is made straight. God is into the details! I thank God Dan's heart surgeon is into the details too. See how the Lord was revealing what He had already spoken? The Holy Spirit reveals all hidden truth and shows us things to come. (See John 14 through 16)

Mother and I went home to spend the night to get rest before the next big day. The surgery was scheduled for later in the morning but I received a call from a nurse asking me if I could be there in thirty minutes due to a change in schedule early that morning. Mother and I both got ready and made it from Lake Norman to the hospital in record time. The surgeon advised Dan they would not do anything till he had gotten in touch with me and we had arrived.

Once we got there we learned the scheduling staff had simply made an error in the time due to the scheduling center being at a different location and miscommunication. *The heart surgeon had the right time all along.* The Great Heart Surgeon—God, has the right time all along too, but there is nothing like getting your adrenaline going first thing in the morning with an early morning change of plans.

I thank God for the heart surgeon, his wisdom and the gift God has given him for the saving of lives. What a gift from God! Thank God for His plan in our lives that He brings to fruition as we trust Him.

We walked with Dan as they rolled him back for surgery. After we walked as far as the operating room doors, we came out to the waiting area where we were surrounded by friends and family. My stepdaughter and her cousin went to set up a scrabble game to keep their minds occupied in a different location where they initially met a security guard named Daniel. He was the nicest man and stopped by each day to say hello and check in on us. This was all part of God's plan too! He connects us with people on purpose.

I have to say that the hospital staff and physicians were exceptionally nice. Due to our lengthy stay at Mercy, I think we met quite a few of them too. From the parking lot attendants, security officers, cafeteria staff, to medical staff and the President of Mercy, I think we met most of the people over the twenty-five day period. We had 25 days in Mercy. I walked by the Mercy Seat daily. Thank God we did not give up on the 19th day of praying and kept our trust in God.

Dan was in three different rooms, and two different Intensive Care units during his stay over the twenty-five day period at Mercy Hospital. Dan had been talking with me about doing full time ministry and getting his business to the place where he could be gone more to help in ministry. Little did he know that he would be flat of his back at Mercy for 25 days sharing his testimony and witnessing the divine intervention by God in his life and sharing it as well.

FIRST HEART SURGERY

Dan came through the first surgery on February 29, 2012 well, but I was still concerned about the pleural effusions and had been since I first learned about it on his CT scan. I mentioned it to Dan's cardiologist and his heart surgeon a few times. I just didn't have peace about this at all.

The first night after surgery, Dan was in excruciating pain. The surgeon told us it would be like getting run over by a Mac truck and it was the toughest surgery anyone would ever go through. I remember specifically him telling Dan not to try and be a hero and to simply stay ahead of the pain with the medications he prescribed.

I prayed and asked God to send angels into Dan's room. Believe it or not, his first nurse's name was Angell. Her name was spelled differently, but needless to say, we had our angel. I was not really surprised by God's confirmation of my prayer. He always goes over board to make sure we are aware of His divine presence. God is just like that! He gives us natural manifestations to assure us of His involvement when we pay attention. I can only imagine what some might think after waking up in recovery and seeing a nurse who said her name was Angell.

FOR SUCH A TIME AS THIS

The second night after surgery was quite interesting as well. While we were eating in the cafeteria, the Lord drew my attention to the monitor on the wall that was showing the word "Purim" on March 8th, which is removal of pain from oppression as in the book of Esther. As you can imagine, the first name of the nurse for that evening was Esther. Do you see how God was bringing constant reassurance of His divine presence?

God was also showing us the removal from pain and deliverance. Stay tuned as you see how God used the name Esther to bring further revelation concerning the vision God gave Melanie about the Mylar balloon at 6:30 AM on February 24th. Esther means *star* and is Persian in origin.

As a matter of fact, the way God spoke to my heart to give our ministry a name was to shorten our name to Star. Nobody knows how to spell Starczewski or pronounce it. Some have even chosen to say it as it might sound in the south. However, when we travel, people in northern regions know how to pronounce it.

The night we had Esther, a new patient was admitted and she had to take over that person for a different nurse. We got a new nurse whose name meant peace, but that was not exactly what we experienced in the natural. I knew God was speaking to me not to leave Dan's side and to be his advocate.

God had given a vision to Melanie that she had shared in-depth with me about Dan. It had to do with a Mylar balloon and an event we hosted on February 11th at The Village in Concord, North Carolina. I will share the details a little later in the book. If you want to look ahead, you can. (See God's Link-Chapter 15)

WATCHING

Mother and I spent almost every night beside Dan during his stay. His surgeon encouraged us to go home but we didn't really want to leave. We would go home about four in the morning to shower, change clothes and return to sit with him.

One night we did go home as three faithful people asked

to sit and watch for us in three shifts so we could get some rest in our own beds. It was quite interesting. When I woke up at home I felt exhausted, but while I was at the hospital with Dan I felt restored and refreshed. God brought people in real pain and real heartache in our path. We met some of the nicest people who had sick family members, some dying, and some in for testing. We met lots of great people at the hospital as we waited, watched, walked by the Mercy Seat, and prayed for Dan's total healing.

Thank God for His mercy and unfailing love during this time. It is actually a miracle that Mother nor I got sick ourselves, as we didn't get too much sleep each night. God supernaturally sustained us through this time as we submitted to the Father.

Dan was extremely uncomfortable so we would be attentive to turning him and helping him all through the night and day. We were right where God positioned us. Dan wanted to be repositioned every minute it seemed. He simply could not get comfortable. Most people wouldn't be able to get comfortable in a hospital bed for that long either.

CHAPTER 10

WORDS OF INSTRUCTION

A STRANGE WORD OF INSTRUCTION

On March 5th the Lord spoke a very funny, yet strange, word to me. When I went home to shower and change, He spoke to me to put on this winter sweater I have that has ribbons with two balls made of fur that you tie into a bow. He whispered to my heart that I would need to have balls that day and stand up to people. I know that may sound a little strange, but that is how He got my attention.

Before I could ever get back to the hospital, Dan phoned me and said in a weak voice, "I'm not sure I am going to make it today with this nursing assistant—can you please hurry back." She either hadn't been informed of Dan's recent surgery or didn't like her job. Needless to say, wherever you have people you will have problems. There are no perfect organizations. Some are short staffed due to economic changes, sickness, or other unforeseen reasons. People simply have to learn to work together. If you stay in any organization long enough, you will experience problems. That's life.

I had noticed the ADVOCATE LINE that was written in chalk on the board in Dan's room so I simply called it to find out what was going on. I met with a nurse who assured me she would look into the problem. I also began to pray that God would send an advocate to the hospital to speak to the staff to remind them of the importance of their jobs and people.

Interestingly enough, I learned that Sorrel King, the mom who started the Advocate Line many years ago, came and spoke to the staff the next day. The Lord Himself is our advocate and sometimes we become an advocate for someone else; especially those we love.

We understand it is impossible to go through life and not experience challenges, people having bad days, lack of communication or small miscommunications. That is part of life and you have to deal with it. In any organization, you will experience issues. Where you have people, you will have problems. Mercy is a great organization and the one God chose to bring healing to Dan.

The Lord also gave me the scripture: "I prepare a table before you in the presence of thine enemies" (see Psalm 23:5) and spoke to my heart to read Psalm 69:16-22.

"Answer my prayers, O Lord, for your unfailing love is wonderful. Turn and take care of me, for your mercy is so plentiful. Don't hide from your servant; answer me quickly, for I am in deep trouble! Come and rescue me; free me from all my enemies. You know the insults I endure—the humiliation and disgrace. You have seen all my enemies and know what they have said. Their insults have broken my heart, and I am in despair. If only one person would show some pity; if only one would turn and comfort me. But instead, they give me poison for food; they offer me sour wine to satisfy my thirst. Let the bountiful table set before them become a snare, and let their security become a trap" (Psalm 69:16-22 NLT).

After looking back in hindsight, Dan and I both now know there were many in business that hoped he died so the truth would not be found out about business issues during his hospitalization. However, God exposes all hidden truth and shows us things to come. You find out a lot about people and where their heart intent lies when they are faced with responsibility. You also find out who your true family and friends are — and the intent of their heart when you walk through a valley.

It *felt* like we were being attacked on every side. Have you ever felt like that? I bet you have if you are still alive. If you read the Bible, you will find that most had the same experiences. Welcome to real life — mountaintop experiences and valleys in between.

WARNINGS OF IMPENDING DANGER

The next day was March 6th. That morning Dan was complaining of a headache and said he felt anxious. I asked his nurse to check him because I knew these were warnings of impending danger as these symptoms may indicate a stroke after surgery. She came in and gave him anti-anxiety medicine.

Later in the morning, Mother and I drove home to shower and change. Again, the Lord spoke to my heart a strange instruction. I had been wearing casual clothing but this day He spoke to my heart to wear a black skirt and white blouse with a black sweater because I would have to step into His authority.

I simply obeyed and started back to the hospital. At 1:33 PM my daughter-in-law Stephanie phoned to ask where we were. She had come to sit with Dan in our absence. Dan had asked her to call me because he felt like he was blacking out and wanted me to hurry and come back. I told her I was three minutes away. By the time I returned, Dan thought he was in the hospital for our son Landon and had no idea he had gone through open-heart surgery. He was talking incessantly and making no sense.

I asked Dan a few questions and learned he thought we were married only five years. I could tell he had short term and some long-term memory loss. I asked him who the love of his life was and he replied, "You and Jesus." I said, "Right answer, there is hope yet!"

I began to pray and spoke words of faith over him. I also began to say "He has the mind of Christ" and I told him he would live and not die. I wrote a series of events on the board in Dan's room and went over and over it again with him for 24 hours. The Lord showed me we had an open heaven over us and our hope was in Him.

I wrote the following on the board for Dan:

LOVE2DAN
Admission 2/24/12
SURGERY 2/29/12
Episodes 3/6/12 (two 2mm infarcts to frontal lobe of brain)
1:33 pm phone call to me with dark curtain and feeling of blacking out

STOP SIGN – Stop Worrying
MEMERE-J (Mind and memory of Jesus)

He asked the same questions over and over again. I kept pointing to the board and telling him the series of events, over and over for twenty-four hours. Thank God the Lord restored Him. It is only the healing power of God that can do that.

I wrote the signs on the board for Dan to see that God had given to us as we walked through this life and death crisis. The day Dan had the two strokes, Melanie was driving and one of her children had to stop to use the restroom. She had to unload all the kids to walk with her little girl. This walk positioned her to see the sign: MEMERE-J and she immediately thought of what I had told her to pray: THAT DAN HAS THE MIND AND MEMORY OF JESUS CHRIST HIMSELF.

Yes, God can go to unusual measures to get our attention if we are open to see with His supernatural vision. God is into the details and He likes to make Himself known, on purpose.

I realized *why* God had said surgery would be like it never happened. Wow! I am thankful God did not give me all the details about what was to come on March 6th. The two strokes are what caused Dan not to remember having surgery on 2/29. Are you starting to see how the Holy Spirit reveals all hidden truth and shows us things to come? It's amazing to me!

On March 7th, Dan had a cardio-version procedure and got a PICC line to clear up pleural effusions and receive nutrients. He was put on TPN a couple days earlier and had an induced fast of five days. (TPN is Total Parenteral Therapy and is given when patients cannot or should not get their nutrition through eating. It is also used for people undergoing major surgery). (Cardio-version can be done using electric shock or medications. It is a method to restore an abnormal heart rhythm back to normal.)

We had to lighten the air a little with the intensity of the situation. I reminded Dan how Jesus was led into the wilderness by the Holy Spirit where He did a forty day fast. Thank God Dan's fast was only five days. You have to find a way to have a sense of humor in life—even in adversity.

THREE FRIENDS

Friday night, March 9th, three men came and sat with Dan all night in shifts. One was our son Landon, and the other two were great friends. Thank God the three friends that came and sat with Dan did not reason and try to figure out why life was happening like Job's three friends in the Bible. God sent great men of God to be by Dan's side so we could take a break for one night. I stay amazed at how God positions people and how He uses the body of Christ to encourage us through valleys.

Thank God for family and the family of God. These three men didn't reason with Dan or try and explain why this was happening. They sat with Dan, talked with him and watched while he slept. They didn't question God—they just watched and sat with Dan to give us a night of rest for eight hours. Always cherish family and close friends.

You will have few in life. Please—cherish the people God places in your life. Friends can sometimes be closer than family.

On a spiritual note, the three friends in the book of Job that came and sat with him represent your mind, will and emotions. All three can run wild unless you choose to continue in your relationship with Jesus Christ through abiding in His Word and having your mind renewed by the power of the Holy Spirit. You see, you can sit in church your whole life and never have encountered the Lord's presence, the person and power of Jesus Christ.

A LITTLE CHECK IN MY SPIRIT —PLEURAL EFFUSIONS

I didn't have peace about the two tubes in Dan's body and had not had peace since I first learned about the pleural effusions. I know the heart surgeon got a little aggravated with me about my questions—but he was the surgeon and I was not. It's wisdom to ask questions.

Not having peace about something is like having a little check in your spirit—that something is just not quite right.

Dan's surgeon told me to stop searching on the Internet,

but what he did not fully understand was that God placed the sense of urgency in my spirit about the problem—not the Internet. I didn't try to explain it to him because there was no reason.

I knew what God was showing me and it didn't really matter. The surgeon sat down with us one day and asked me to stop doing research or he wouldn't be so nice the next time. I silently prayed and asked the Lord to touch his heart. Then he told me he was just kidding. That might not be the exact words, but the point is, the Lord was revealing all hidden truth.

The next morning, he came in the room and said he could hear my voice talking about the pleural effusions as he came across the parking deck to the hospital. He then explained he had to do a second surgery due to a problem with the effusions not clearing properly. I admire this surgeon and his ability to communicate with total strangers in such intense times of life and death situations. *Thank you to this special surgeon for not giving up on Dan's life and for having a heart of understanding.*

HEART CHECK:

Ask God for help when you have a problem. Don't hesitate to ask. The secret is to trust God with the information that comes. Gideon did not trust, so he asked again in Judges chapter 6. God graciously provided another sign for him. God still speaks today through His Word, dreams, visions, signs and wonders. He speaks through His still small voice and can even use a child to speak to you. Don't be surprised at how God may speak to you. He goes to extreme measures to get our attention.

Ask yourself this question: Do I have a heart that hears when God is speaking?

CHAPTER 11

SECOND OPEN-HEART SURGERY

The second open-heart surgery was on March 13th, 2012. He had to have a second surgery due to the pleural effusions not clearing up properly. I sensed the spirit of death and didn't have a good feeling in the pit of my stomach. I chose not to talk about it but instead, chose to believe God and ignore the devil. The Lord also gave Melanie a dream about how she was warned the enemy was trying to take Dan out early through death. She came to the hospital early that morning to go to the Chapel to pray. I sent her a text on her phone to let her know where I was waiting in the hospital. She later told me the little waiting room where we were was exactly what the Lord had shown her in the dream.

God speaks to His children and shows us things to come. He gives visions and dreams. We can see but God gives vision. God was not just speaking to me, but others around us as well. He is no respecter of persons. He wants us all to hear and know His voice.

Dan was in recovery for longer than expected. One of the hospital attendants had advised me she would take me back shortly. An hour or more passed yet again with no sight of her. I got up and walked over to the information center to inquire. One of the caregivers saw me and said she would take me back. As we walked to recovery there Dan was with a Bi-Pap machine on because his $Co2$ levels were not rising to normal levels. My dad died with a Bi-Pap machine on and the enemy was trying to get me into fear.

I gave Dan a hug, kissed him, told him I loved him and went out to pray. The Lord spoke to me to go and sit on the rock sculpture. This is the first time I learned what it was named— *"The Mercy Seat."* God was showing me an open heaven over us where His healing was flowing to Dan in Mercy. I sensed the Spirit of death but refused to give into fear. Thank God for His grace and mercy and the hope He gives us to believe.

Dan was sent to Intensive Care after surgery and was spared again. I asked his surgeon if he would walk with me and talk to me for a few minutes about Dan. I simply wanted to know his thoughts on Dan's situation. I wanted to know the bottom line. He assured me he would walk with us through this difficult journey *and he did just that.*

We walked through great challenges, but God positioned great people to walk with us! I thank God for the surgeons and medical staff he positioned with us. Challenges of life can shake your confidence. We were certainly living with challenges, but chose to have hope in God. You can too with whatever you are facing!

You can have God-confidence that is the absolute assurance that God can and will accomplish whatever He wants through whomever He chooses. God has a purpose for your life and is more than capable of seeing it through to completion. Ask the Holy Spirit to develop an unshakable confidence in the God who loves you! God was making Himself evidently clear to us at Mercy Hospital.

Self-confidence looks inward. God-confidence looks upward. Where is your faith? Where is your trust and assurance? Is it in people or God? Pay attention as you read and learn to trust God in your current challenge or life situation.

More days passed and more waiting. Dan was scheduled

for a cardio-version on the morning of March 20th, but God had a different plan. He put Dan's heart back into rhythm Himself. Watch God at work again!

HEART CHECK

Tips to sustaining a healthy heart:

Check your own heart daily for any signs of an unforgiving heart—and *choose to forgive*.

Lift your broken heart to God and ask Him to heal it—if necessary, do surgery.

ART of MERCY

"*Mercy Seat*"

*Created by renowned artist
and craftsman, Michael Sherrill*

Media: Silica bronze, natural stone and porcelain

CHAPTER 12

GOD'S INTERVENTION

D an had already had a cardio-version during his stay. He was scheduled for another one on March 20th first thing in the morning — we all thought.

On March 19th, the Lord gave me an interesting vision at 11:30 PM of Dan being charred or burnt. The next morning we learned that just before midnight, the Lord Himself had put Dan back into normal heart rhythm. Dr. Bower could tell the time it occurred as he looked at the monitoring system.

The vascular surgeon team came in to check on Dan. Then Dr. Bower came in and sat down on the side of Dan's bed. He told us Dan seemed to go into normal heart rhythm on his own just before midnight. I explained to him about what the Lord had shown me. Another time, we were amazed at the power of God and He revealed He was taking care of Dan Himself. At times in our lives, we all need a touch from God.

Psalm 16 (NLT) "Keep me safe, O God, for I have come to you for refuge. I said to the Lord, "You are my Master! All the good things I have are from you." The godly people in the land are my true heroes: I take pleasure in them: Those who chase after other gods will be filled with sorrow. I will not take part in their sacrifices or even speak the names of their gods. Lord, you alone are my inheritance, my cup of blessing. You guard all that is mine. The land you have given me is a pleasant land. What a wonderful inheritance!

I will bless the Lord who guides me; even at night my heart instructs me. I know the Lord is always with me. I will not be shaken, for he is right beside me. No wonder my heart is filled with joy, and my mouth shouts his praises! My body rests in safety. For you will not leave my soul among the dead or allow your godly one to rot in the grave. You will show me the way of life, granting me the joy of your presence, and the pleasures of living with you forever."

HEART CHECK

Ask yourself these questions:

How is my heart?

Am I where I need to be in my walk with God?

CHAPTER 13

THE HOLY SPIRIT IS OUR GUIDE

O ne morning a preacher on the television was talking about how Jesus walked in resurrection power here on earth and it seemed General Patton walked in the same gift with strategic details. Think back to how God speaks about the artisans in the Old Testament. On that same morning, I heard another minister share his testimony of how God supernaturally brought in the finances for a need of over 3.5 million dollars.

I believe and know that you can see better with your heart than you can with your eyes. God gives us vision when we learn to see with our spiritual eyes of understanding from a heart like His. The Holy Spirit is also a faithful guide. God has not left His children helpless. He provides us with the Holy Spirit as our guide who knows the way in every detail.

"When the Spirit of truth comes, he will guide you into all truth. He will not be presenting his own ideas; he will be telling you what he has heard. He will tell you about the future" —John 16:13 NLT

HAVE YOU NOTICED?

The Holy Spirit led Jesus into the Garden of Gethsemane. It was part of the Father's plan.

Have you ever felt like you were in your own Garden of Gethsemane, facing a hardship or extreme circumstance? Obviously, Dan and I had to put our faith and trust in God as we walked through this journey at Mercy. I believe we must get to the point where we are transparent enough to share our faith in Christ with others to see His resurrection power manifested in our own personal lives. You can simply be who God created you to be and also be transparent enough to share what you're walking through so others will notice.

There was a naked boy in the Garden of Gethsemane. Who was he? Have you ever noticed this scripture before? Let's read it together: "And there followed him a certain young man, having a linen cloth cast about his naked body; and the young men laid hold on him: and he left the linen cloth, and fled from them naked" (Mark 14:51, 52 KJV Camb.Ed.).

We learn through the Gospel of Mark there was a naked young man found in the Garden of Gethsemane just after Jesus finished healing the ear of the servant of the high priest named Malchus. Why was this young man following Jesus and who on earth was he? Have you ever thought about this? I wonder why on earth the Holy Spirit inspired the writer to include this very unique story in the account of Mark—why is it significant? Perhaps you think as I do and are wondering the same thing.

I believe the linen cloth had everything to do with it as Jesus was wrapped in a linen cloth. If you study the Greek, the particular word that is used for this "linen cloth" is used in only one other event in the New Testament. This depicts the "linen cloth" in which the body of Jesus was wrapped for burial. (See Matthew 27:59, Mark 15:46 and Luke 23:53)

This is the only reference found for this particular kind of cloth in the New Testament. It is a burial shroud used for covering a dead body in the grave. Do you suppose this boy came out of a grave? Was it the resurrection power of

Jesus? His naked body wrapped in the "linen cloth" reveals the man's identity.

We have been to Israel several times and know a little about the Garden of Gethsemane. It is situated on the side of the Mount of Olives. It also has a gate around it and it is an extremely populated cemetery. When Jesus said, "I AM," the power that was released was so phenomenal that it threw the soldiers backward and obviously created a rumbling in the cemetery. This young boy was raised from the dead.

I believe this young boy followed Jesus to see who on earth had that kind of power to raise him up, don't you? The word here for "followed" actually means to *continuously follow*. This tells me that the resurrection power of Jesus is supernatural, raises us up from the dead, raises us up above our circumstances, and creates a desire in us to follow Jesus continuously. Do you have that desire? Who are you following? Are you condemning those that God has placed in your life or are you gaining wisdom?

Oliver, our next-door neighbor's cat comes over to visit us each day to eat treats—I have to tell you, he is getting fat. His owner laughs about it. There is something interesting to note here. When we choose to connect with others who are full of the Word of God and love Jesus, we will increase in wisdom and understanding too. We will get fat in the Word of God. No, *not* fat in body weight—but in wisdom. Who you choose to connect with is vitally important.

I am extremely thankful for the power of God that raised Dan up and gave him another chance to live again! Dan doesn't mind telling his story now either. He is unashamed of the power of God and has an amazing testimony of God's miracles in his life. Are you ashamed of the gospel of Christ?

The Bible tells us that when the soldiers reached out to apprehend the young boy, he broke free and fled, leaving the linen cloth behind. This is a type and shadow of what Jesus did as He walked out of the tomb. When we follow after Jesus continuously and abide in His Word, we can break free from the enemy's hold on our life as well. We won't be deceived or distracted anymore. We will recognize enemy tactics.

As we reflect on His amazing power, that same power is active today. We know later in the Bible, Jesus told Pilate, "... Thou couldest have no power at all against me, except it were given thee from above..."(John 19:11 KJV). The presence of Jesus was so great that no one could withstand Jesus if He had chosen to resist, as Jesus was taken by the will of God not the will of men. Jesus *gave* His life that we would have that same power available to us through His resurrection. He is seated at the right hand of the Father and we are seated with Him in heavenly places. *Are you beginning to grasp the power available through the Holy Spirit today?*

How marvelous and how wonderful it is that Jesus gave His life for you and me! No one had forcible power to take Him except it was the Will of His Father. Take a leap of faith today and trust God in greater measure for the details in your life. What are you needing God, the Great "I AM" to release from you presently? Is it a financial, emotional, relational, or physical problem?

The Holy Spirit trains us to hear the Father at the slightest whisper at the door of our heart so we will obey instantly for the saving of lives, both spiritually and physically. Military are trained in the same manner. We are in a battle here on earth, but the victory is ours through Jesus Christ, the living Word.

STRATEGIC TRAINING

We can draw close to the Father, like Jesus, and learn to hear strategic instructions. I love history and learned General Patton had a strong courage and unusual boldness and confidence, as it appeared he received strategic instruction from God. He must have committed his army to the Lord. His superiors thought he was crazy, but if they had listened to him, communism would have been wiped out during World War II because he wanted to have his troops go into Russia, take Russia and defeat Stalin, the communist leader for Russia.

General Eisenhour, who was a five star general and leader of the forces during World War II in Europe, refused to listen to General Patton. General Patton wanted to continue riding through Russia into Moscow to get rid of Stalin and get rid of communism. The Chief of Staff and other authorities thought Patton was nuts.

When we receive wisdom from God, the people around us may think we are nuts too. The world does not always understand the things of God. Whatever we commit to God, He will take care of ---so what is our problem? It may be your health or the health of someone you love, it may be your finances or even fear of losing your job or career. It may be your fear over the recent turn of events in America and across the nations. Whatever the case, God cares!

What have you *not* committed to God? I chose to commit Dan to God in this life and death crisis! Look at what the Lord has done! Run to Jesus and lay your cares out before Him in prayer:

LORD,

You are so amazing and I love you so much! Thank you for giving your life for me that I may be free for all eternity. Thank you for the Holy Spirit. I thank you from the depth of my heart for loving me just like I am right now. Help me to grow and have greater understanding and wisdom in every detail of my life. I boldly declare that I am valuable and precious in your sight. Amen.

Also, pray and ask God to give our government leaders wisdom, from our President right down to the leaders in our cities. Pray for those in authority and practice showing respect and honor yourself.

In Matthew 26:57, the Bible says, "And they that had laid hold on Jesus led him away to Caiaphas the high priest, where the scribes and the elders assembled."

After Jesus exhibited His phenomenal power, He permitted the soldiers to actually take Him into custody. Have you ever felt like you were a prisoner in any area, perhaps your emotions? In a particular sense, this was an *act* because He had proven they did not actually have adequate power to take Him. The words "laid hold" are from the Greek word *kratos* and the word means *to seize, to take hold of, to firmly grip, and to apprehend* in this particular case.

Once Jesus made it obvious He could not be taken by force, He allowed the soldiers to seize Him. Matthew 26:57, the Bible says they "led him away." This phrase comes from the Greek word *apago*—the same word used to picture *a shepherd who ties a rope about the neck of his sheep and then leads it down the path to where it needs to go.* This word also pictures exactly what happened to Jesus that night in the Garden of Gethsemane. He was not dragged to the high priest as one who was resisting arrest. The Greek word *apago* very plainly and strategically tells us the soldiers slipped a rope about the neck of Jesus and led Him down the path as He followed behind, just like a sheep being led by a shepherd.

The Bible confirms Isaiah 53:7 because the Roman soldiers and temple police led Him as a sheep to slaughter. The soldiers led Jesus to Caiaphas the high priest. Do you know much about Caiaphas? I did a little research to gain understanding. We know that he was appointed high priest in the year 18 AD. Even when his term ended, he still had great power and influence in the business of the nation, including its spiritual, political, and financial affairs. The famous historian Flavius Josephus reported that five of Caiaphas' sons later served in the office of high priest.

Caiaphas married Anna, the daughter of Annas, who was serving as high priest at that time at a very young age. Annas served as the high priest of Israel for nine years. They kept the power in their family for many years. After Annas passed the title of high priest to his son-in-law Caiaphas, Annas continued to manipulate and control through his son-in-law. It was actually a spiritual monarchy. As holders of this great title, they held great political power, had control over public opinion, and owned vast amounts of wealth.

This influence is recognized in Luke 3:2, where the Bible tells us, "Annas and Caiaphas being the high priests..." It was not possible for two people to serve as high priest at the same time, but we see Annas clearly held much power and authority. He was extremely influential to the very end of Jesus' ministry when those who arrested Jesus in the Garden of Gethsemane led Jesus to Annas first before presenting Him to Caiaphas, the real high priest in position (John 18:13).

They were both Sadducees, a group of religious leaders who were very doubtful of the power Jesus held and were more consumed with doctrine and tradition than the supernatural power. With the constant reports about the power Jesus held and the news of miracles, the Sadducees viewed Jesus as a potential threat to their positions. They were apparently control freaks and in constant competition. When they learned of the resurrection of Lazarus, they absolutely flipped out and simply decided to get rid of Jesus. They were filled with rage and were worried about the growing popularity of Jesus. Does this sound vaguely familiar today? They held a secret council to decide if Jesus should be killed. Caiaphas was the one who ultimately decided how Jesus was to be killed. He was also responsible for arranging the fraudulent and illegal trial for Jesus before the Jewish authorities. He charged Jesus with blasphemy and Jesus would not contest the accusation Caiaphas brought against Him. Then he was delivered to the Roman authorities. They found Jesus guilty of treason for claiming to be king of the Jews. After the death of Jesus, Caiaphas continued to persecute believers in the Early Church.

Jesus had never sinned (2 Corinthians 5:21); no guile was found in His mouth (1 Peter 2:22); and His entire life was devoted to doing good and healing all those who were oppressed of the devil (Acts 10:38). It does not seem fair that Jesus was led like a sheep to slaughter in the midst of a group of spiritual vipers in authority in Jerusalem. Does this seem fair or just to you? Not me!

Our precious Lord Jesus yielded Himself to the Father who judges righteously. He is our Abba Father. This week I came upon a car with the sign *ABBASGRL* (Abba's Girl or daddy's girl). I knew God was trying to get my attention. Next, I saw a sign on a car with the word: "Panoplia." It means:

1. Full armour, complete armour.
   a. includes shield, sword, lance, helmet, greaves, and breastplate

See how God positions us to see His signs to us for our security in Him. We can "STOP WORRYING." Are you getting it friends? Whether it is a health issue or a government issue, when we know who we are in Christ and submit to His authority, we can cast our care upon Him and rest in His victory.

HEART CHECK

Ask yourself these questions:

Do I worry and fret?

Do I have peace?

Do I submit to and respect authority?

Do I see the blessing of God in my life?

Ask the LORD to help you submit to proper authority and to learn how to pray. Pray and ask God for His wisdom and for the Holy Spirit to teach you. Surrender and submit to His authority.

CHAPTER 14

SUBMISSION AND SURRENDER

Jesus submitted Himself to the Father. He understood submission and authority. A person who understands authority will experience miracles as Jesus did. The apostle Peter wrote about Jesus: "Who, when he was reviled, reviled not again; when he suffered, he threatened not, but committed himself to him that judgeth righteously" (1 Peter 2:23 KJV).

Let's take a look at the word committed here. It is the Greek word *paradidomi*, a compound of the words *para* and *didomi*. The word *para* means *alongside* and carries the idea of *coming close alongside to someone or to some object*. The word *didomi* means *to give*. When these two are together it is the idea of *entrusting something to someone*. The prefix *para* depicts that this is someone to whom you have grown extremely close and have an intimate relationship or fellowship. It is very close. It can also be translated *to commit, to yield, to commend, to transmit, to deliver,* or *to hand something over to someone else. This is what I had to do with Dan at Mercy; obviously, I was not in control.*

You may be in a situation that is unfair or unjust and you feel like someone needs to be dealt with but it is out of your hands. I beseech you to draw near to the Father and choose to commit yourself to His tender loving care. He wants the very best for us. As I think about just how intricately detailed

God is and how He orchestrated every minute of our days in Mercy Hospital, I stay amazed and in awe of His tender mercies and extravagant love. He manifested Himself to us in ways that go beyond what words can articulate.

You may be in a predicament that has left you feeling hopeless to perhaps feeling angry and bitter over a situation where you know you did everything in your power to make it work, but it didn't. We still have hope in Jesus! Jesus was severely mistreated when He was arrested and it seemed there was no escape for Him. He was in a position where He had no choice but to trust the Father. This is where we are today---where we must also trust The Father. Pray the following:

Lord,

When I find myself in situations that seem unbearable, help me look up and see my strength in You as I walk through each day. When I am tempted to retaliate, help me remember Jesus. I declare by faith that I can STOP WORRYING because my Heavenly Father is taking care of every detail in my life. When I am tempted to be filled with anxiety, help me rest in the knowledge that You will take care of me. I declare that I rest in You, LORD. Even when I am in a situation that is unjust and unfair, I know that God is at work behind the scenes turning all things out for my good and His glory. He loves me with an everlasting love. He cares for me. I am extremely valuable to God and He desires the very best for me. In Jesus' name, I pray.

CHAPTER 15

GOD'S LINK

This is the account of the vision God gave Melanie about the Mylar balloon I mentioned earlier.

SERIES OF DOCUMENTED TEXTS OF EVENTS

I have waited on purpose before sharing this part of the series of events that occurred in my husband's life. If I had written this in the beginning, you may have been prone to doubt. I wanted to build your faith to believe that God still speaks. And, He will connect you with people that He speaks to as well and that want to grow. Get a clue! God still speaks!

Let me share how God connected us with Melanie and her family. I will simply include what she wrote:

I had gone to a women's retreat at church. You could choose from several different topics that our church had speakers lined up for that Saturday morning. I chose "Hearing from God" and it was being taught by Deborah Starczewski. I didn't recognize the name or face. As soon as she began talking, I felt a connection to her. I was absolutely amazed at her stories of how God spoke to her. Then she began to tell a story about her son Landon at a wrestling match and how God had given her a vision of him being seriously hurt by this wrestler. It was at that moment, my jaw dropped. I needed to meet this lady!

For as long as I can remember, I have gotten visions of things. I never really understood why. Some things were really bad, some things good, and some things were just weird. I never really thought much of it unless the vision was bad. I would rebuke it and do my best to forget it.

Through Deborah telling her story, I realized that God was showing me things in the supernatural and that he wanted me to take action. That action for the most part would be PRAYER! GOD WAS SPEAKING TO ME! WOW!

I wanted to know more! When Deborah finished speaking, it was premature for me! Women swarmed around her and I had to get home to my baby daughter. I was so sad that I didn't get to talk to her, but I knew God would take care of it.

On Sept. 11, 2011, I found out at 4:00 PM that Deborah was speaking at our church that night. My husband had to take my son to ball practice that night and there was no way I would be able to stay the whole time. It didn't matter to me! I went for as long as I could. Once again, she opened my eyes and explained what God was doing personally to me and through me. I had never heard anything like this, AGAIN! Once again, I had to leave without getting to speak to her. Come on!! Ok God, I trust you...

A couple of month's later, right before Thanksgiving, a friend and I were giving a baby shower at the church. Well guess who walked in the door, DEBORAH! God connected us that day and the anointing began flowing immediately! God actually woke me up that night telling me Deborah was trying to contact me. I blew him off. I said, "God, it is 3 in the morning! I just met her this morning! She is not trying to contact me!" Sure enough, I got up that next morning and there was a text from Deborah at 3:15 AM! Deborah is an amazing woman of God. I have learned more in the past year from her mentoring than all of my thirty years in church. She speaks God's love and truth everywhere she goes and truly has a heart for reaching this hurting world. I am so thankful for her and all of the work she does to further her FATHER'S kingdom!

—Melanie Campbell

This gives a recap of how God connected us.

Now, let me give you a recap of what happened.

On Monday, February 20, 2012 Melanie sent a text to me to ask how Dan was feeling. I sent a text back saying: Dan is worse—are you filled with the Spirit? If so, pray in tongues. Melanie immediately responded she would pray.

Melanie began driving to her next destination and praying in the Spirit for Dan. Her eyes were drawn to a car parked on the side of the road because it was what her family had wanted for the last two years. It was a pearl Cadillac Escalade and had a sign on it: STAR1. She was praying for Dan—and sometimes people call us Dan Star or Deborah Star because our name is Polish and sometimes difficult for most to spell or even say correctly. She also knew our non-profit ministry is Star National Outreach Worldwide and knew God was confirming to her that He was hearing her prayers.

I sent Melanie a text on Friday, February 24, 2012 at 5:40 AM in the morning to ask her to continue to pray as we were headed to the hospital for two procedures. I explained Dan didn't want everybody to know until the doctors determined what was necessary. I asked her to pray in agreement with us for Dan's total healing, for protection and God's hand HIMSELF to do the procedures. I let her know we were to be at Mercy at 12 Noon—and that Dan needed heart surgery.

Melanie sent a text at 6:14 AM: I have been praying nonstop for you and Dan. God is the healer of broken hearts!

Melanie put her phone down, shut her eyes and began to pray. About a minute into her prayer, God showed her a vision. She said she saw her and I in a wooden room with the floors, walls, and ceiling all being made of wood. She saw me standing at the back of the room where there was a double doorway at the entrance that was open to the outside with this bright light from the outside shining into the room. Melanie indicated we were both busy doing something and then all of a sudden, she saw a Mylar balloon floating into the room. It was four times the size of a normal Mylar balloon. The balloon was VERY deflated, almost to the point that it didn't look like it should be floating. There was also very large black lettering in a foreign language on the balloon. There were three words with 3 to 4 letters in each word. The words were located in the middle right, middle left and bottom of the balloon. The balloon floated in the door to the middle of the room. Then it began to lift up towards the ceiling. Melanie said she looked over at me and saw that I was looking up at the balloon also. She said she saw a perplexed look on my face and the vision ended.

Melanie opened her eyes in shock. She went downstairs and began to tell her husband what had just been revealed to her. Melanie thought the lettering appeared to be Chinese but that it was not. She only remembered 2 letters for sure. One looked like an H but with two lines crossing through the middle and the other one looked like a slanted 7.

I thought they were Hebrew letters because the Lord had given me a dream of a Hebrew letter years earlier. The Lord had impressed upon my heart to attend a prophetic conference in Greensboro. I chose to go and the speaker put the Hebrew letter the Lord had given me on a visual for all to see. I knew the Lord was leading me and showing me something specific. I explained this to Melanie and told her to research Hebrew letters. *I look back now and realize, yet again, the Holy Spirit was training me then for today.*

Toby, Melanie's husband, told her to look up different languages on the Internet. She found what appeared to be Hebrew letters. The only problem was that what she actually saw had dots or periods above and below some of the letters as well. She prayed and asked God to reveal all hidden truth and continued to pray for Dan. At the time, Melanie was nervous to tell me about all this because she didn't understand what God was revealing.

Little did she know, that God has given me the gift of dream and vision interpretation—that only come from God. Sometimes we don't know what other people know. God knows how to connect all the dots and He knows who to position us with to help us grow and mature in Him.

About 12:41 PM, she sent me a text with all this information about the vision from God. I began to pray and came against all foreign objects of darkness and thanked God for His breath in Dan. Melanie called and told me she was overwhelmed with emotions and inquired if Dan was in surgery. I explained he was only having a TEE (trans-esophageal echo of the heart) and a heart catheterization.

Dr. Bower had informed me they would schedule surgery Monday or Tuesday unless it was urgent that day. I remember sharing about the red balloons we had at our most recent event on February 11th about the Love of God, a teaching on the book of John—and we had John Love and his band do worship with John sharing his testimony.

God had spoken to my heart to teach on the book of John and God's love for an event for Valentine's weekend. One of the ladies in our Sunday morning class called me to tell me she didn't want to miss our class but wanted to hear a young man who was going to be speaking and singing that same day. I told her to go! After she shared a little of this man's testimony, I assured her that she should connect with him because God may use him in her own family.

Believe it or not, God not only connected her with John

Love but with us as well. Nobody but God could orchestrate an event where He specifically spoke to my heart to teach on the book of John and love and have a singer named John Love who I would later meet. We hosted him and his band for our event on February 11th, 2012 at our home church. Are you starting to see how God designs each day and gives you confirmation along the way?

My red heart helium balloon from the event was still up and beautiful at home. As a matter of fact, it never deflated fully, even after two months. I actually had to press the air out of the balloon in order to put it up for safe keeping as a reminder that our breath of life comes from God. It is only God who determines our number of days.

I asked Melanie to keep praying and saw the significance of the Mylar balloon in the ancient lettering.

Earlier, I shared how Dan went into heart failure during the heart catheterization and was admitted to critical care. I explained he had to get stable enough for heart surgery. Melanie later told me this scared her. She was at church watching her kids and a pastor's kids while her husband was in a coach's meeting. She was supposed to go to Ladies Night Out directly after the meeting was over, but sensed in her spirit there was no way she was doing this but instead, was going home to pray! Later Melanie told me she was emotional and the vision God gave her she felt like was a bad sign.

She phoned me to ask if I needed anything and let me know she was going home to pray. I shared with her that Dan was in critical care waiting to become stable enough for surgery. We talked about the details a little and I shared with her that Dr. Bower told me Dan was alive because of my persistency and that Dan should be thankful he has a persistent faithful wife.

PERSISTENCY

Persistency is key in life. Dr. Bower told me Dan was alive because of my persistency and that Dan should be thankful he has a persistent faithful wife. We all have to be persistent and keep moving forward. We must choose to be faithful. It is a choice. Life is full of choices. You may be facing one right now and reading this book. You may feel like you are at a crossroads and don't fully understand what is going on around you. You may have waited too long to take action or ignored God's warnings. You may be angry with yourself for waiting too long to take action. Whatever the case, God is still faithful—even when we are not.

Be encouraged to believe again and keep your trust in God. Whether it is your health, relationships, or finances, God still has a plan. He has a great plan even if it looks like a life or death situation. I believe God trained me not to be afraid of people or their opinions on purpose. If He had not done so, I might have been reluctant to move so quickly or believe what God was speaking to my heart. He trains us to hear and obey for the saving of lives!

On February 25th, that Saturday morning about 1:24 AM, I sent a text to Melanie asking her if she found out what the Hebrew letters meant. I sent a text asking her if a Mylar balloon is helium filled—and aluminum. Because I know God shows us things in the natural to make us aware of what is going on in the Spirit realm, I pay close attention to details. I stayed awake watching Dan's monitors.

Sometime later, Melanie reminded me about the dream of the balloon. She said it was very deflated but still rose up slowly after it got in the middle of the room and in the dream, I had a confused look on my face. Looking back now, I realize the balloon was a representation of part of Dan's heart and we were in the middle waiting for Dan's body to become stable enough for surgery.

Many friends, family and church family were praying around the clock for us. It was obvious there was a battle going on for the life of my husband. Thank God for His divine intervention and for prayer.

Melanie sent me a text the next morning and let me know she woke up with God asking her a question. This is how He gets our attention to move. God asked her what a star was made out of and kept showing her the word "star" everywhere she went. She knows our ministry is Star Ministries and Star National Outreach Worldwide is our non-profit, so she looked it up on the Internet and found this:

A star is made up of 2 main gases, Hydrogen and Helium. When a star is "born," it is predominately made up of Hydrogen. As it grows old, Helium will increase. When a star is dominated by Helium, it goes out and is the end of the life of the star. Then she researched the contents of a Mylar balloon and learned it is made of Nylon. Nylon consists of dominantly Hydrogen, but also has carbon dioxide, oxygen, water, and salt.

The vision God gave her started to make sense. The Mylar balloon represents Dan STAR, consisting of Hydrogen and Helium. Since a Mylar balloon and a star are made up of hydrogen and the balloon she saw had very little helium because it was so deflated, this was a good thing! If a star has very little helium in it, it has a lot of LIFE left in it! Wow! It was then 7:24 AM on Saturday, February 25th. We had done our research—all we had left was the Hebrew lettering.

We most likely looked like a tired bunch and I am quite sure most did not see all that was going on behind the scenes, but we certainly knew God was at work with all the details of hope He was giving us. We were in a life and death situation and chose to believe God for a miracle because it is His power that raises us up and gives us life—see Psalm 71:20 NLT. God is the restorer of life.

Some people choose to ignore the details because they think it is too much work. When you choose to turn aside and see God in the details, He makes Himself evident. Moses had the same experience. God has not changed. (See Hebrews 13:8)

Interestingly enough, the Hebrew lettering she saw in the vision was the same lettering used on the first set of Ten Commandments that God gave Moses. God never ceases to amaze me.

Melanie and I talked about the Hebrew lettering and I told her to search it out on the computer. There's not much you can't find out when it comes to research. She typed in "History of Hebrew" and found a website that explained Old Hebrew did not consist of vowels. "But what about the lettering?" Melanie asked God.

The website Judaism 101 Hebrew Alphabet, quotes that Hebrew literacy declined, particularly after the Romans expelled the Jews from Israel, the rabbis recognized the need for aids to pronunciation, so they developed a system of dots and dashes called nikkud (points). These dots and dashes are written above, below or inside the letter, in ways that do not alter the spacing of the line. Text containing these markings is referred to as "pointed" text.

Melanie was so excited. She had found the dots and what a God moment. God gives us wisdom when we ask and search. She couldn't remember all the letters, but there again, God speaks in part and He knows our limits.

On March 5th, Melanie found the letters she had seen in the vision God gave her. She found it on the website, www. teachinghearts.org and learned that the Hebrew alphabet had changed over the years. The script she found her letters in was K'tav Irvi (Ancient Hebrew Script) and meant fence in, hedge, chamber, separate or hedge of protection. The Gimel means camel, deal, recompense, Lift up—the deflated balloon LIFTED UP.

You can see through the details that God is always at work giving us hope in Him. The more we turned aside to look, the more God revealed to us that He was divinely involved.

We must choose to worship God in the midst of everyday life. Life is full of seasons and we have hope in God. We must choose to worship God in the good times and in the difficult. The Holy Spirit is always at work in our lives. We just have to take the time to notice and express our appreciation through worship.

CHAPTER 16

THE HOLY SPIRIT
AND OUR GIFTS

The *Holy Spirit wants the gift of you.* I want to recap about a most amazing act of worship and extravagant gift we find in the pages of the Bible. This will enable us to see more clearly where we are in our own life, our own attitude of heart, and our spiritual location at present. We can choose to worship Jesus right in the middle of the most adverse circumstances.

Jesus wants us for Himself. God is deeply interested in a love relationship with us. I had selfish reasons for wanting my husband to live. He is my husband and very precious to my heart. We love spending time together. There is no one else that touches the heart like a spouse. I wanted Dan to live and I knew we needed the Holy Spirit's help and power to heal Dan. I remember asking Dan who the love of his life was and his answer was, "You and Jesus." This was right after he had two mini strokes and I was checking his memory. He had the perfect answer. That was his heart response. When we are born-again, that is our response as well.

God is first and foremost, then our spouse. I was more concerned about Dan based on our relationship than for any other purpose. I wanted him to live.

Christmas can be a prime example of where we stand in relationship to God and others. Do you want more of God

Himself, or do you simply want what He can give you? Do you only visit family to see what you might get as a gift or do you like spending time with them? Do you secretly care more about money or census than you do the heart of the matter or people themselves? Do you only want to be in business when things are going good or do you bail out at the first sign of a problem, shunning responsibility? If this is your heart, it is hardened and needs healing. As a matter of fact, you might not even be truly born-again or saved at all.

We are not saved primarily to serve God, but we are saved primarily because He wants us for Himself. That is why He has *"loved back our lives from the pit of destruction and cast all our sins behind His back"* (See Isaiah 38:17). I believe this is why Moses who received the law saw the behind parts of God and we see Jesus.

The Bible never once tells us to do anything *for* God. It tells us God chose us to involve us in what He is doing through His love and grace. We can work with Him and allow Him to work through us.

The Bible is very clear in revealing our first obligation as a Christian—it is ministry to the Lord. Much like Mary with the oil of spikenard, we too must be filled with the Holy Spirit (represented by the oil), mixed with the Word (Jesus) and the Blood He shed on the cross for our salvation in order to have power that leads others to Him.

In Genesis 1:1, we see God first moved by His Spirit; then He spoke the word, and all things came into being. (See Genesis 1) In Acts 2, we see another one of God's patterns. Pentecost is actually the record of the first time the Holy Spirit was poured out *"upon all flesh"* (Acts 2:17) and not just on prophets, priests, and kings, but *"all flesh"* means men, women, children, and regardless of age or status in life.

When we study the Word closely regarding the Holy Spirit, we find that God used men and women to utter praises to God first, then He used Peter to preach the Gospel to several thousand people. The key to worship is giving something to God. Worship is tied closely with sacrifice. Worship came first and witness to mankind followed.

Though the word *worship* is not particularly used to describe Mary's act in John 12, the story of her offering gives us an absolutely remarkable example of worship. I believe it came from a heart of abandon to the Lord Himself.

Like Mary, when we kneel at His feet and pour out our worship in ministry to Him, then He comes to us and the very fragrance of His presence fills the sanctuaries of our lives. (The Bible records the ointment was "costly").

I remember some time ago when my mother and I both had food poisoning and were violently sick, I was so exhausted I could hardly walk to the bathroom. I remember smelling the fragrance of the lily of the valley fill the bedroom in the early hours of the morning. I knew the Lord Himself made His presence known and we were going to be fine.

A few weeks before, the Lord started speaking to me about the Lily of the Valley. One morning I noticed I had a bottle of shower oil that was named "Lily of the Valley" a dear friend of mine had given me for my birthday years before. The fragrance was still just as strong as the day I initially opened it. A few days later, I found a jacket in my closet with the same flower design that I had never worn. Yes, it was the Lily of the Valley. God was preparing me to recognize His presence when he entered my room that night when I was violently sick with food poisoning. I had spent a few hours in the emergency room with my blood pressure at 40/32 with nurses running to and fro around me as it continued to drop. Thank God for IV's. God went to extreme measures to show me he was paying attention.

THE RESURRECTION POWER OF GOD

The story of Mary's offering of worship gives us an example of a heart of adoration. Jesus speaks of an incident where he describes as good work in Matthew 26, Mark 14, and John 12. Jesus declared that wherever this gospel is preached this woman's act of worship will be told as a memorial to her. What was it and who?

Lazarus has been raised from the dead by Jesus. Many of the Jews who had visited Mary of Bethany had also seen the things Jesus did and believed in Him. Some went away simply telling the Pharisees about what Jesus did. (Study John 11:47-57)

Lazarus had been raised from the dead and a feast was being held at Bethany for Jesus, who is the Resurrection and Life. They were all eating and drinking together with Jesus and the glory of Christ was manifested among them. In resurrection from the dead we behold the glory of a new creation, the goodness of God, and the rest, satisfaction and joy of God, as well as peace, joy and righteousness in the Holy Spirit due to the glory of resurrection being foreshadowed.

The resurrection power of God still works today! Thank God for His power so graciously exhibited at Mercy on behalf of Dan for 25 days. Wow! What a modern day miracle. Miracles still happen daily. Worship God no matter what. We witnessed the power of God and our greatest tool of evangelism is our testimony. This is worship unto God. What we experienced at Mercy is not just for us, but for all to know and understand that God is still alive. Take a leap of faith and dare to believe again. We all need hope. Jesus is our Blessed Hope!

CHAPTER 17

VICTORY IN JESUS

W e can surmise from Scripture either waste or worship when we observe the details in the life of Mary. Martha worked, Lazarus witnessed and Mary worshiped. The resurrection of Lazarus, followed by this supper with the One who is the Resurrection and the Life, leads to a new act of worship. We find worship is always the essence of the glory of God. (Read John 12:1-8, Mark 14:3-11, and Matthew 26:6-13)

When we learn to listen to the promptings of the Holy Spirit we can live in victory in every area of our life. I believe when we know the truth of God our worship changes. When we have been delivered from much, our worship is fueled with gratitude, joy, brokenness and reverence. When we are more conscious of Jesus than we are of our failures, we worship freely because we understand we are forgiven. The love of God is the demonstration of His forgiveness. His love empowers us to worship in an attitude of being totally sold out to Him, no matter the personal cost.

The death, burial, and resurrection of Lazarus gave witness that the wound to Israel was incurable and Israel must die. The old way is incurable, sick unto death, stinking with decay. That is the state of mankind without the hope of resurrection through Jesus Christ.

When we see Jesus, we are changed. The glory of God is manifested where God's nature, His being, is satisfied, and brings about overflow in the Spirit realm that manifests in the natural. He desires that we correspond as He draws us to Himself.

When Jesus took Peter, James and John to the mount of transfiguration—they saw His glory. Moses and Elijah appeared—revealing we no longer listen to the law and prophets, but we look directly to Jesus. Peter's name means stone, James means to replace and John's name means grace. The stone (or the law given on the stone tablet) has been replaced by God's grace. Law is replaced by grace. Jesus is greater than the law and the prophets. Jesus came and touched them. He told them to arise and not be afraid. The law condemns the best of us but grace saves the worst of us.

We are called to be living stones that exhibit the Grace of God wherever He positions us. I believe that is why the Bible says, "even the rocks will cry out." We are called to be a witness of the power of God in our everyday lives. That is what we were doing at Mercy—as we kept waiting on God's timing and seeing His hand at every turn. After Dan's surgery, I had two of my favorite men with On-x in their hearts. Landon has an On-x valve and Dan has the On-x ring, the surgeon used to repair Dan's heart.

God also spoke to me that no one would ever come against us and win. He has sealed our marriage with His divine ring that man cannot destroy. When someone comes against us, they are coming against God Himself. He is our guard. He is our very present help in times of trouble. He reveals all hidden truth and reveals the intent and motives of people around us. He will show you as well, if you will pay attention.

When you choose to spend time in the presence of God, whether sitting in a hospital, reading your bible at home or driving to work in your car; you too, can experience the glory of God. You might wonder how on earth can one have an intimate relationship with God and hear Him in the details. He has not changed. He spoke to people in the Old Testament and in the New Testament. Let's reflect on the life of Moses. The face of Moses shown with the glory of God and Moses saw the back parts of God. When Moses came down from the mountain the people ran away in fear. When Jesus came down the mountain the people ran toward Him. The people immediately saw Him and saw the glory. (See 2 Cor. 3)

People saw the power of God at work in Dan's life during his stay at Mercy Hospital. Dan gave Him praise and shared his story with all that came to see him. God is still the same yesterday, today and forever. (See Hebrews 13:8)

The Spirit gave us Grace. On Mt. Sinai the Law was given and 3,000 died. Grace came on the Day of Pentecost and 3,000 were saved. The law demands and commands. Grace says it is done – grace imparts. Jesus revealed Himself. God is the lifter of my head. Amen.

When we see Jesus we are changed. We are empowered to worship because of intimacy and knowing we are forgiven. Where grace reigns there is increase in every area of our life. We are free to worship Him. When we see His hand in our personal life, we are forever changed and have a new level of trust like never before!

Lazarus died and we know from Scripture he was buried and left beyond any doubt of his death. Jesus came and raised Lazarus from the dead in a profound and prophetic action of hope for all humanity. Praise God.

At Mercy Hospital, there is no doubt about who brought about the healing in Dan's life. He used doctors and surgeons, but He is the ultimate healer. Miracles are a testimony to the power of God and bring glory to Him.

The devil hates to see Jesus glorified. Satan will do anything to steal our worship. Satan will do anything today to receive worship. He does it in all sorts of forms and subtle ways. He moves through media and tries to steal the hearts of children, youth, adults and entire generations. It is time we pay attention to the warnings of God and choose to take a leap of faith and believe Him again. I pray that God instills hope in you as you read this book and that you will learn to look for God in your everyday life. He will open your eyes to His resurrection power all around.

Resurrection and ascension means that the entire ground of Satan has been set aside and nullified. All things are Christ's. We know from Scripture Satan is filled with pride and his desire is to have everything for himself, to be as God, to be the seat of knowledge, and to find a place of worship in the heart of every believer.

One thing the enemy hates is meekness. He is nullified by meekness because it destroys the very ground of Satan's authority. Paul was a meek man but if you don't understand the biblical meaning, you will miss the point.

The Hebrew word translated "meekness" is *anav* or *anaw,* meaning "depressed (figuratively), in mind (gentle) or circumstances (needy, especially saintly): humble, lowly, meek, poor" (*Strong's Exhaustive Concordance,* #6035). The translation depends upon the context in which it appears. The *Gesenius Hebrew-Chaldee Lexicon* adds, "afflicted, miserable; commonly with the added notion of a lowly, pious, and modest mind, which prefers to bear injuries rather than return them" (p. 643). The *Theological Wordbook of the Old Testament* indicates why this word is so difficult to express as a single term: "anaw expresses the intended outcome of affliction" (p. 1651).

Meekness can appear bold and courageous because it is eternity minded on all points. Paul, Moses, Jesus Christ, and David were among the meek. Jesus Christ never sinned but we know the others did, and so do we. God sees the condition of our heart. He will use circumstances to reveal what is in our own heart and allow things to happen that spur us on in His perfect plan. Everyone will not go where God is calling you to go. He gives people the opportunity to repent and then He removes people from our lives so we can move onward with them or without them.

God trained me to stand in the gap for Dan. He taught me not to be moved by fear or opinions of others. God will train you specifically for the task set before you, whether it is standing in the gap in prayer for someone in a life or death situation, or simply a matter of believing God for a wayward teenager. God loves us so much that He still speaks and wants us to take *a leap of faith* to simply believe Him.

This is a prayer the Lord spoke to my heart to write and send out to our intercessors:

— — — — — — — — — — — —

WE are so eternally thankful that the Lord has the POWER to put an end to all our problems! We thank GOD that we rest in HIS POWER and HIS ALONE for all eternity in every detail for each day. WOW! We experienced that daily by the second at Mercy Hospital. HIS love is amazing. HIS mercies do not fail. Bless His Holy Name!

Lord, help us to be efficient and help us not to waste time and energy. We ask YOU to speak to our hearts with specific instructions to tell us what to do, where to go, then HELP us follow through at the whisper at the door of our hearts to the very letter of your instructions. We thank YOU for the patience as we watch YOUR ALMIGHTY HAND supernaturally work behind the scenes and to our "watchful" eye as YOU allow us to see through YOUR EYES.

We boldly affirm and declare that JESUS CHRIST has the power to fix all our problems on a daily basis. Life has just enough problems to keep us ever depending upon the Lord. Amen. We REST IN HIS POWER and HIS GOODNESS because HE LOVE US with an everlasting love and with loving kindness HE has drawn us to HIM. Wow! What amazing love GOD has for you and me!

We turn to the LORD and thank Him for His wisdom, insight, power and the detailed answers we need to get from where we are today to where HE is instructing us to go. . . .right down to the smallest detail. . . .to where we need to be in HIS divine purpose.

I thank God for His ministering angels protection, provision and placement for every minute of each day. We declare by faith that His mighty power works through us, that His divine power is being released right this very minute to destroy the enemy at work behind the scenes, to tackle every problem we encounter in advance and for HIS peace in every situation.

The LORD spoke to my heart that HE trains us for war. We are trained as military as Generals in the Army of God so that we will live and teach others to hear HIS voice at the slightest whisper at the door of our hearts. This is so we obey HIM instantly. THIS is for the saving of lives, whether spiritually or physically. Amen. GOD is the Master teacher and Lord of our lives.

He woke me up at 4:11 AM to come downstairs and send out this prayer and letter. Sometimes the Lord gives us an instruction that saves us. Whether it is someone lurking in the streets and suddenly the light comes on in the home to delaying us five minutes to miss a car accident. HE is amazing. I love him and HE loves us. How on earth can I ever thank HIM enough for saving my precious husband's life...so when HE wakes me up, I love to obey Him.

Lord, I pray you never let me forget your incredible love for me and I never want to get to the place where I ignore Your divine interruptions and interventions. I thank the LORD HE keeps us on fire with HIS burning fire that never goes out, straight from HEAVEN, so that we fan the flame in others for the Lord. Amen.

JESUS willfully demonstrated HIS love on the Cross at Calvary for each of us. Lord, help us to never forget that! JESUS demonstrated and exhibited this recently in a powerful way for us. We are seated in heavenly places with the Lord. Let's not ever forget that!

Dan and I have our own resurrection story now since GOD raised Dan up on February 24th and gave Dan a new lease on life. Wow. What an amazing display of the power of God. I want to be excited forever about the details of God's hand in my life. May we live like new believers with great love and joy for the Lord, but like the Lord Jesus in wisdom, insight and understanding for every situation we encounter. May we be so full of the love of God that people can sense HIS presence when we walk by. Amen.

We boldly declare HE loves us. He loves you dear prayer team! He took our sin! He carried our sickness; and He bore our shame on the Cross. Because of HIS amazing redemptive love, we are saved, healed and never need be ashamed. WE are saved, sanctified and not ashamed. Amen!

Thank YOU for your continued prayers and faithfulness.

Love you all,

Deborah

CHAPTER 18

SITTING AT THE FEET OF JESUS

G od loves us with an everlasting love and with loving-kindness He draws us. I believe God loves a heart that worships Him. He longs for us to spend time in His presence. God gives us a view of His love when we choose to sit still long enough to hear and see.

Dan had many days at Mercy to spend in reflecting on what God was doing in his life. We were not so concerned about normal life stuff, but life and death. Life stopped for Dan as he knew it—and God positioned him where he would be saved from early death.

Let's take a little closer look at Mary of Bethany, a woman who along with Martha and Lazarus is deeply loved by Jesus. She sat at the feet of Jesus, was born of a woman and anointed by the Spirit of God. Mary of Bethany demonstrates her deep desire to be joined to Jesus through a demonstrative act of love, a gesture of lavish, abandoned devotion, literally, a beautiful act of worship.

Mary took an alabaster jar filled with costly spikenard and anointed the head and feet of Jesus. "Spikenard" means "glistening." The Bible says: "While the king is at his table, my spikenard sends forth its fragrance. A bundle of myrrh is my beloved to me; that lies all night between my breasts. My beloved is to me a cluster of henna in the vineyards of

En Gedi (SOS 1:12-14 NKJV). This is a picture of the soul's intense thirst for union with Christ. Ask yourself this question, "Do I have a thirst like that for Jesus?"

It requires spikenard—the outpouring of one's life. It requires myrrh, the spice of burial and wealth. (Crucifying our flesh daily and giving) The vineyards of En Gedi bring to my mind abiding in the well that springs forth into everlasting life through Jesus Christ. Spikenard strikes the body of sin for death. (Romans 6:6).

What can I learn from this passage about spikenard? What do you suppose those watching were thinking when they saw her tears of adoration flowing on the feet of Jesus? Did they think, "What sin does she have now" to assuming they understood her heart? None of us can even begin to understand the heart of another unless we first take time to get to know them.

We certainly know that the heart surgeon got to know Dan's heart as he performed two open-heart surgeries. God wants us to know Him as well. Over the time we spent at Mercy, we had the opportunity to speak with the doctors more than normal. Dan's surgeon and cardiologists were actively involved in walking with us through this valley. Dan had to choose to participate with them. He also came to know Jesus at a more intimate level with his own resurrection story.

I can see a desire to participate with Christ, not just imitate Him. I can see a desire to partake, to possess the life that is in Christ, to enter into the place of abiding, as well as spiritual oneness with Christ, our vital union. The Bible says: "We are made partakers of Christ." (See Hebrews 3:14)

The call to spikenard is a call to participate in Christ's death, as His death is our death and pays the penalty, so is His resurrection our resurrection in the days to come. By one Spirit we are baptized into one body (1 Cor. 12:13) and joined unto the Lord to be one spirit (1 Cor. 6:17). One might ask, "How?" The answer is this: we lay down our life to serve Him. Spikenard cost an entire year's wages. It is a representation of all that you are and do. The costly spikenard might appear to be a waste rather than worship, but that is not the case. We lay down our lives, our reputation, our own agenda, our self and we live to glorify God. We lay down our life because we realize we are dead in trespasses and sins. You choose to willingly die to the natural carnal fleshly ways and acknowledge the sin of being double-minded.

In 2 Samuel we find that like David, Mary of Bethany, would not give to the Lord that which cost her nothing (2 Samuel 24:24). Mary of Bethany is found three times in the Bible at the feet of Jesus (Luke 10:39, John 11:32, John 12:3). Like Mary, we must listen to His Word. I can just imagine seeing her basking in His presence as she clung to every word He said, can't you? She sat at His feet because she wanted to be close so she wouldn't miss a thing. That is how we must choose to live our life, even when others watching don't understand.

She poured out her sorrow and grief as she fell at His feet when Lazarus lay dead. This was an ultimate act of worship. It is not wrong to pour out our grief; it is sin to stay in grief. Like Lazarus, we too must die to self. Sometimes, God removes people and things from our lives that can't go into our future with God. He prunes us over and over again throughout life. *He is doing that in America today. He is constantly doing that in our lives as Christians.*

Mary fell at the feet of Jesus to pour out her sorrow. There are times as children, teens and even adults that we need to pour out our sorrow to God as well. I was talking with a teenager today who was so broken over his father not wanting anything to do with him, that he fell on the floor in tears. He was so upset and heartbroken that he stayed home from school. I talked with him and prayed with him. He was feeling the pain of rejection and abandonment. I don't understand how a good father can do this to a son. It is not normal. People get blinded due to sin and hurt others.

At times in life, we can feel sorrow and grief. We can feel refreshed, worn out, or have a loss of strength to move on in different circumstances. We can be devastated at the loss of a spouse, a child, or even a job. Can you imagine how Mary felt about Lazarus? When Lazarus died, she said, "Lord, if you had been here, my brother would not have died" (John 11:32 NIV). Lazarus is at the celebration supper. He was brought out of the grave by Jesus and out of the grip of death. He had been loosed from the grave clothes and is seated with Christ at supper.

As believers, we are seated with Christ in heavenly places (Eph. 2:6) to enjoy basking in the presence of Jesus, fellowship and food. Lazarus is a living witness as Mary demonstrates an understanding of what is required. She lets her hair down and wipes the feet of Jesus with her hair as well. She takes the place of a servant. In untying her hair she does something Jewish women did not do in public (1 Cor. 11:15). She dismantled her own glory. She chose to humble herself in an outward act of worship through public, spontaneous, sacrificial, personal lavish outpouring of adoration for her Lord. She was not embarrassed nor was she ashamed to demonstrate such a love for Jesus.

HEART CHECK

Ask yourself these questions:

Can I sit quietly and read the Word of God?

Am I able to listen to what God wants to say to me?

TIPS: Try keeping a journal and writing instrument beside you. Simply jot down any thoughts that come to mind until you get quiet and can focus on Jesus and His Word.

CHAPTER 19

SALVATION AND ANOINTING

S alvation is a free gift from God but the anointing has a cost. Mary wanted more than just the free gift of salvation that was paid in full by Jesus dying for her sins and taking her punishment. She recognized that Jesus became sin for us. She chose to be sold out to Jesus. I have to warn you that this kind of relationship and this level of worship will bring criticism, even from others that are close to Jesus.

Judas called her worship "a waste." Since Judas was the treasurer, he apparently snubbed his nose at her in self-righteous indignation. He thought his criticism was valid. He seemingly appeared devoted to the natural concerns of the poor but really wanted the spikenard given to him instead. The Bible records the first words we have of Judas: "Why was this fragrant oil not sold for 300 denarii and given to the poor?" (See John 12:5)

We find his last words recorded: "I have sinned by betraying innocent blood" (Matthew 27:4 NASB). Judas *was* the treasurer, but Mary chose to put her treasure into the Kingdom of God that no one comes to steal. I have to warn you that greed cannot understand giving. Greed only understands taking. Familiar words you might hear are: "What is in it for me?" Scripture indicates Judas apparently thought he was poor as he was justifying stealing and taking for himself.

Those who see themselves "wealthy in God" because

He owns the hills and all the cattle on them can give freely because they see themselves as children of the Most High King. Jesus took on poverty that we might have wealth in God as El Shadai. This wealth the world does not understand. The Holy Spirit reveals all hidden truth and shows us things to come. The Holy Spirit reveals the motives and intents of the heart. The Holy Spirit certainly revealed Himself and showed us things to come on a daily basis at Mercy.

There will always be people that don't understand you or your relationship with Jesus. I am sure there are probably some at Mercy Hospital that did not understand us. There may be some in our own church where we worship and teach that don't understand as well.

Judas was a thief and he thought Mary's act of worship was irresponsible wastefulness. Judas later calculated a bargain with the religious leaders to betray Jesus. It's only about money, a deal, a sale or a profit to the heart of a thief. A thief doesn't want to take responsibility but wants everything given to them. They want something that cost them nothing.

This is also happening today in America and across the nations. Needless to say, with the change in economic conditions across the globe, I am sure you have seen the demise of integrity and people doing things you would not have hoped or expected. People sometimes measure and are selfish.

Mary was obviously uncalculating in her giving. She was generous and Jesus did not condemn Mary; He blessed her. Mary blessed Jesus and He blesses us. There is no anointing or glory without suffering. The love of God is a perfecting love, not a love that pampers. The Bible tells us Jesus was perfected in obedience through the things He suffered. What are you suffering through now? What is the condition of your heart?

The first gift we give is our self. We must choose to give self freely to Christ.

We know the resurrection of Lazarus by Jesus precipitated the arrest of Jesus and the events we call "holy week" today. The anointing of spikenard prepared Jesus for His death and burial. Jesus tells us this Himself. The beautiful fragrance that filled the room announced to the spirit world that Jesus would pass through death to life, that He would be the offering that would be pleasing to God. He is the very fragrance of life to those who are called to life in Him and the fragrance of death to those destined to die.

Can you imagine the sweet smelling fragrance that filled the room that day? Can you close your eyes and sense the awesome presence of Jesus right now? He is still waiting right now for us to enter into His presence, even today, at this very moment in time.

This supreme act of worship through the spikenard represents a life poured out to God. There is a higher calling—one of total surrender and worship. Mixed with Jesus' Blood and the spices of myrrh and aloes, the fragrance says to each of us, here on earth and all in heaven, that Jesus is Lord over death! Mary heard the call and chose to arise!

Mary of Bethany had a disposition to die with Christ, for it was the way to glory. The higher call of this supreme act of worship is actually a call to prepare oneself for death and burial, not a fleshly act but a divine dying. Let death work in you. (See 2 Corinthians 4: 10-12) Sacrifice is actually an offering up, not a giving up. It is a place of total surrender— the offering up of life. Will you give your life up to live with Christ?

When we choose to plant ourselves in the likeness of His death, we shall also reign with Him in His resurrection. If we suffer with Him in this life, we shall be with Him in the likeness of His resurrection. Ask yourself this question, "Do I delight in this spontaneous act of worship?" Jesus calls it a "good work." Jesus says it will be remembered forever and told.

The higher call, the call for spikenard, is a call to a decision and a determination to worship Jesus in spirit and in truth. The Bible depicts the self-life, fretful, self-centered, greedy, hateful, envious, duplicity and superficial phony devotion through the life of Judas. The spirit of Judas is still alive in people today.

God is calling today for us to die to sin, to self (Romans 6:11), to die to the world (Gal. 6:14), to die to the Law (Romans 7:14), and to die to the divisions of man; gender, race, culture, language, etc. (See Ephesians 2:13-17).

When we see the true vision of the greatness of God and the Holy fire of the Spirit that ignites the fire within, our own spirit responds in selfless acts of worship. It is the call to go for it all; to go for the glory with the promise that "to the one who overcomes I will grant to sit with Me on My throne, as I also overcame and sat down with My Father on His throne" (Rev. 3:21 KJV).

Obedience is an act of worship. (See Romans 12:1,2) Worship may come in tears, songs, shouts, heads that are bowed, altars filled with people crying out to God, lifted hands, confessions, acclamations and obedient lives. We will sense a deep longing to know God more intimately. When we meet this man named Jesus and come to see His face, we are changed from glory to glory.

The higher calling, the call for spikenard, is a divine call to present your body as a living sacrifice, holy and acceptable to God, which is your reasonable service. Mary of Bethany obeyed God as she took the spikenard and anointed Jesus Christ.

Spikenard "is obtained from vegetation growing high in the Himalayas and processed after piercing the bark of the plant with a pointed hook-like instrument. Applied to Jesus' feet, soon to be pierced by the nails on the cross, this ointment prophetically demonstrated the pathway Jesus would walk upon to receive the honor due Him" (Page 1385, The Revival Study Bible).

Here my husband found himself in Mercy Hospital flat on his back after telling God he sincerely wanted to do His perfect will in ministry. He wanted to fulfill God's call. God's power and anointing were made present constantly.

The anointing prepares one for the glory of God. The anointing destroys the yoke. Jesus rose from the dead. The anointing consecrates us to the service of God. I believe Mary perceived as she obeyed, for she is not recorded as going to the tomb after Jesus rose from the dead. Unless of course, she is not the Mary we might think.

She is one of the few that is recorded who ministered directly to Jesus. She obeyed God as she took the spikenard and anointed Jesus Christ. The anointing covered Jesus with the fragrance and when it was mixed with His Blood was pleasing to the Father.

We must choose to live in this world but not be consumed by the world. It is more important to be doing things *with God* rather *than for* God. You can be so organized and so consumed with the perfect future you have planned that you miss God's divine interruptions and His perfect will. On the other hand, you can be so double-minded and perhaps floundering about that you never finish anything at all. A combination of working with God brings fruit. Dan could have been so consumed by his own timetable that he missed God's will and died early, but thank God he didn't. Dan chose to obey God in the face of adversity. God allowed him to be positioned where his immediate need was revealed.

Don't get so consumed with the world and the things in the world that you forget the real reason for life—living to serve the Lord and being in relationship with Him. When we pour ourselves out before the Lord, what is dead will die, and what is alive will live. The Bible says: "Be faithful unto death, and I will give you the crown of Life" (Rev. 2:10 NKJV). We must desire to participate with Christ, to know Him more intimately and the power of His resurrection and the fellowship of His sufferings. We must choose to partake.

Choose to believe what God says about you and dream big. God uses those who are available and hear His heart. We hear Him whisper when we stay close to Him. Learn to obey God and what He has placed in your heart. It will bring life and lasting fruit. Do things with God no matter who gets the credit. We must dismantle our own glory, for no flesh will glory in the holy presence of God.

We must choose to die with Christ in order to live with Christ and in Him. Learn to delight in holy worship. This will result in obedience in your walk with the Holy Spirit. Learn to obey the promptings of the Holy Spirit immediately so you can live victoriously in every area of your life.

Live victoriously through selfless acts of worship. Plan a life—plan to live to point others to Jesus through their witness of your life in His presence. Determine to worship Jesus in spirit and in truth to overcome. Live in faith! Live in abandonment to a life of obedience and one without shame and with great faith in your heart that Jesus is the Resurrection and the Life! When we believe in Him, crucified to our flesh, yet living in faith, we are the ones that will never die but reign throughout eternity with Him.

Even when others mistreat you, as they did Jesus, look to the author and finisher of your faith and live an outward expression of selfless acts of worship through genuine abandon and adoration of Jesus Christ.

Notes from study and my findings:

In addition to the mother of Jesus, there are two women who are mentioned repeatedly in the Gospels as being part of the entourage of Jesus. The first of these is Mary from the village of Migdal or Magdala, in Galilee. She is not mentioned by name in the accounts of Mark and Matthew until at the time of the Crucifixion where she is numbered among the followers of Jesus.

She appears relatively early in the Gospel of Luke while He is preaching in Galilee. She apparently accompanied Jesus between Galilee and Judaea. In this culture, it would have been unthinkable for an unmarried woman to travel with a religious leader and followers alone. Jesus was not consumed with what people thought, was He? He met the woman at the well at noonday in Samaria.

When Mary is first mentioned in the Gospel of Luke, she is described as a woman "out of whom went seven devils." Luke and Mark both mention a similar anointment by an unnamed woman, though neither Luke nor Mark identify her with the Magdalen, but Luke does mention she was a "fallen woman." She was also a woman of means. Luke reports that her friends included the wife of a high dignitary at Herod's court—and that both women supported Jesus and His disciples with their financial giving. The woman who anointed Jesus was also a woman of means. Mark stresses the costliness of the spikenard ointment that was used as well.

It is obvious that the anointing of Jesus was of extreme importance. Anointing was the tradition for kings—and in particular for the "rightful Messiah," which means "the anointed one."

I personally believe that when we have a revelation of Jesus Christ and the magnitude of His forgiveness, we too will have a heart for worship and adoration for Jesus. As Simon Peter heads the list of male disciples, we find that Jesus first chose to reveal His resurrection to the Magdalen. Jesus treats her in a very unique and preferential manner as well. I can just imagine this would stir up jealousy in the other disciples. The portrayal of her as being a harlot shows the heart of the people to damage her name, not realizing she was forgiven. Their hearts were in far worse shape than this woman. Sad to say, but this still happens today. The devil and the people he uses are the only ones who remember your past. Sometimes, Satan tries to make you condemn yourself through false guilt and shame. People were jealous in the day of Jesus and envious of her relationship with Him as well. Envy is still alive today. It must die in us as Christians.

No matter the status of the Magdalen in the Gospels, there is another woman who may be identified as Mary of Bethany, sister of Martha and Lazarus. We know this family is wealthy because his house contained a private tomb—a luxury in Jesus' time. This was a sign of wealth and symbolic of their aristocratic connections.

We know that Jesus stayed away a few days with His disciples after hearing of what happened to Lazarus. This would even be a curious delay in our culture. When Jesus returns to Bethany, Martha rushes to meet him, but not Mary.

By the tenets of Judaic law at that time, a woman "sitting shivah" would have been strictly forbidden to emerge from the house except at the express bidding of her husband. We can observe Mary conforms precisely to the traditional comportment of a Jewish husband and wife. Could it be this is a type and shadow or foreshadowing of when the Lord Himself calls us home? We are to occupy until He comes. (www.halexandria.org/dward225.htm) Notes

Could it be that the woman who anoints Jesus is the Mary Magalen? Could it be that Mary of Bethany is the same woman? I don't know. The medieval Church regarded them as such, and so did popular tradition. Many biblical scholars concur today as well. We might observe that Mary of Bethany is not mentioned as being present at the Crucifixion although Mary Magdalen is!

I believe it is of substantial importance that Mary Magdalen was the last person at the cross and the first person to see Jesus after His resurrection. She ministered to Him using her own resources; she anointed Him for ministry and burial, and was most likely on his right hand at the Last Supper. We can observe she was a constant companion of Jesus. Are you?

I certainly know without a shadow of doubt that Jesus is a constant companion to us. It was made evident at Mercy Hospital on a daily basis. God raises us up for His purpose. God raised Dan up for "such a time as this."

Note that Jesus gave to Mary Magdalen and to her alone the commission to preach the gospel. She was even instructed to "go tell Peter" that wheresoever the gospel was to be preached, Mary's love and devotion to her Master were to be declared.

Do you suppose it is possible that her past was sealed because she had been forgiven, like we as Christians are today? Perhaps, she was forgiven much and loved much. Her heart was made evident through her outward expression of a love and adoration of Jesus. I believe Jesus still tells secrets to those today who stay close to His heart.

Jesus told her secrets and she was His beloved. She is a type and shadow of the Church. He is still speaking today as you can see by reading the evidence in this book. He wants you to hope again!

"But I have called you friends, for all things I have heard of my Father I have made known to you" ---John 15:15 NKJV

HEART CHECK

Ask yourself these questions:

Is there anything bothering me?

Focus on your body for a moment. Does anything hurt at all? You have just assessed your own body and emotions. You can see how the Lord has taught me to pay attention so far.

Do I have unresolved issues or do I feel agitated about something that is not resolved?

As you begin to ask yourself those questions, time and

time again, in different situations, you will begin to hear what the Spirit of God is speaking to you. Learn to quiet yourself and cast your care upon the Lord. When you learn to quiet yourself, you will then begin to hear the Spirit of God speaking to you as a believer.

CHAPTER 20

THE SNARE OF DOUBLE-MINDEDNESS

Will you be a Mary, one who gives her best, or do you have the spirit of Judas at work in your heart? Will you believe God in the midst of adversity or will you give in to reasoning? Will you choose to believe God at His Word and trust Him with your life, family, finances, and friends? Or, will you give into reasoning when life throws you a curve ball? When you begin to doubt and reason, you become double-minded.

I thank God He trained me to hear and obey, for *if* I had been worried about what people thought or their faces, I would have accepted whatever was going on and never been persistent. God doesn't want us to sit around and wait. His desire is that we hear and obey, which moves us to action. God trains us much like being in a battle, because it is for the saving of lives, both spiritually and physically. In this case, it was imperative to move things along for my husband. You can't always sit around and wait on someone else. Sometimes it is a matter of life or death.

An individual who is spiritually double-minded is someone who has not made up his or her mind to do God's will, accept God's advice, or believe what God is revealing in any given situation, no matter what it may be. Yes, this person desires deeply to hear from God! However, after you have heard, you will make up your mind whether or not to follow what God is saying. I have to tell you, this is not God's way. The Bible tells us in the Book of James: "If any of you lacks wisdom, let him ask of God, who gives to all men generously and without reproach, and it will be given to him" (James 1:5 ESV).

Let me give you an example. I believe love covers small offenses, but the bigger they get, we are called to confront in love and make a decisive action. Everyone is not going where you choose to go in God. Let me explain. Let's suppose someone has an attitude toward you and says something really wrong. Then, the Holy Spirit speaks *to you* about going to them and asking for forgiveness, confessing your attitude about the wrong without saying one thing about his or her part. In most cases, a spiritually double-minded person would not follow through on this prompting or even carry out such advice.

Suppose it is a huge business matter where you have truly been wronged, much like Judas was trying to do here with the woman that gave lavishly. He wanted what she had rather than her giving it to the Lord. Judas apparently wanted what this woman had for his own. Not much has changed in life through the ages. We can observe this is the marketplace today, in large businesses, corporations and the lives of individuals.

Maybe it's also your opinion of what you may think or feel someone should have done. These are all areas where we dare not tread. God keeps us moving forward. If you are a Christian, stop judging people and stop gossiping. Learn to confront and deal with issues according to God's Word.

I remember hearing an older man making a statement from the pulpit at a conference. He said, "People either want what you have or they want to know what you know and did to achieve it." A wise statement that was and still is today, don't you agree?

We met with my husband's doctor yesterday who was sharing about his oldest son in college and how he is growing up fast after leaving home. He said his son is finding out that you don't just all of a sudden wake up one day and have a nice car, a nice house, and a bank account; it takes hard work. People work hard to achieve goals.

As a parent, we must teach our children responsibility and give them the opportunity to make choices with allowing them to suffer age appropriate consequences; otherwise, they will grow up to be double-minded or expect everything without a cost. *If I had been double-minded at Mercy with regard to Dan, he would have died early.*

People will not always understand your actions. You must learn to make choices because life and death can stand in the balance. There will always be people who question your actions, but you have to learn to operate in the wisdom of God and not the fear of man.

Judas did not like how Mary gave her best to Jesus nor did he understand why. He obviously thought it was a waste. He must have had different ideas in his own mind. He wanted it all. He didn't like what this sister was doing with her resources! She lavished her gifts upon Jesus! Nothing is wasted when given to Jesus! Not even our pain! As you can see from God's divine intervention in the life of Dan, it is wisdom to make the right choice.

HEART CHECK

Ask yourself these questions:

Am I a double-minded person?

Do I reason and doubt God?

Do I have a spirit of deception at work in my heart?

Have I been deceived to think God doesn't see my hidden sin?

God is at work in each of us on a daily basis. Study the book of James. James reminds his readers that the Holy Spirit desires for us to be faithful. We remain faithful when we humble ourselves, admit our wrongs, and resist the devil. God desires that we draw close to Him so He can purify us by His Spirit.

"They can't make up their minds. They waver back and forth in everything they do" —James 1:8 NLT

CHAPTER 21

THE BIG PICTURE

When Dan told Dr. Bower he wanted to wait till after April 15th to have surgery, he was obviously not seeing the big picture. Sometimes we don't see clearly. Sometimes we think we know what is best or better, but we are wrong. Things aren't always as they seem.

Let me share a story. On another note, a dear friend of ours was sharing about her little girl. Her parents were repainting her "big girl" room and she wanted it purple. I believe purple is for royalty, don't you? She is a little princess and all girls are in the eyes of God.

We are children of the Most High King and receive His royal blood at salvation. We all have to grow up and regularly have our heart and mind cleansed through the washing from the Word—Jesus. God is our Father, Jesus is our elder-brother and the Holy Spirit is our teacher, guide, comforter and best friend who warns us and prompts us to obey the Lord. Much like the little girl's daddy was priming her bedroom walls, Jesus still does the same today on our journey of growth and maturity in Christ.

Her daddy was priming the walls and she woke up from her nap to come and check out the progress. She stood at the door with her hands in her pockets saying, "Daddy, I said I wanted it purple. This is not purple." What the little girl did not know was that her daddy knows best. He was priming the walls with white primer for the coat of purple. This is much like our lives as a believer. Our Daddy God has to white wash us first before we can receive His royal benefits. What do you suppose God is priming in your life today? He is always at work in our heart. Whether it is open-heart surgery, or God doing spiritual surgery, He is still at work within us.

God invites us to ask Him for wisdom. He also gives us a warning: "But let him ask in faith without any doubting, for the one who doubts is like the surf of the sea driven and tossed by the wind. For let not that man expect that he will receive anything from the Lord, being a double-minded man, unstable in all his ways" (James 1:6-8 KJV).

The way to overcome double-mindedness is to first acknowledge your own fears. You must be determined to do something about it and realize you, alone, are responsible. Doubts and vacillations are sin and clearly wrong. Acknowledging this to God will open the doorway of escape from the snare of double-mindedness.

You may believe God one minute and doubt the next. This is double-mindedness. Choose to believe God and dare to dream for more. There is always more in God. He has greater things planned than you can dream or imagine. Choose to take a leap of faith and hope in God again. *Have childlike faith and step out to serve God in the big picture.*

HEART CHECK

Ask yourself these questions:

Do I have childlike faith to believe God?

Do I have pride in my life and think I know better than God?

What does God want to prime out of my life?

Have I missed the big picture of eternity or am I so focused on life that I don't see the hand of God at work in my own life?

Pray: LORD, help me to see clearly and be eternity-minded always. Amen.

CHAPTER 22

WHOM DO YOU SERVE?

You and I are faced with the same decision with which Joshua confronted the children of Israel: "And if it is disagreeable in your sight to serve the Lord, choose for yourselves today whom you will serve: whether the gods which your fathers served which were beyond the River, or the gods of the Amorites in whose land you are living; but as for me and my house, we will serve the Lord" (Joshua 24:15).

Let's read a promise of Jesus: "If any man is willing to do His will, he shall know of the teaching, whether it is of God, or whether I speak from Myself" (John 7:17).

When there is a vacuum from not hearing the voice of God Himself, the enemy will speak words he wants us to hear instead. Sometimes the enemy will say exactly what you want to hear so that it may position you for your own purposes or desires. You and I must deliberately choose to do what God says whether it lines up with the purposes of our own heart, our own agenda, or interrupts our day. We must choose to be sold out to Jesus and single-minded toward God. Would you be willing to give God a signed check today and allow Him to fill in the blank of what He would have you to do?

What will you do with this book and the divine intervention of God that you have just read? God brings each of us to the cross, which presents us with a crisis—to believe or not believe. *Take a leap of faith and dare to believe again!*

What will you do when God places it in your heart to give your all like Mary of Bethany? Will you give it freely in the face of opposition, when others think you are wasting your resources on God's Kingdom or will you succumb to peer pressure and miss God's best? How will your heart respond to a Mary in your presence?

Will you choose to tell people about God's intervention while you are walking through adversity or will you moan and complain? Thank God for Dan's heart, for God's divine intervention, and for all the people God used in the healing process. Dan had told God he wanted to do full-time ministry and he ended up in Mercy Hospital. How we respond to adversity tells us where we are spiritually.

Where are you? Do you enjoy what God is doing in your life and through you? Do you know Him personally? Maybe God has placed a particular believer in your life that makes you think differently about life. Don't think that is coincidental.

DIFFERENT GIFTS

Is it possible that to be a Mary you need a Martha? There is a business side in life and even in ministry. There is a business side to healthcare. We first see Martha worried and busy doing much with Mary at the feet of Jesus. We see Lazarus was raised from the dead and delivered. Perhaps, once we have sat at the feet of Jesus, we begin to do things with God as He has called us to do. At the hospital, Dan needed the surgery and He needed God. We needed others to stand in agreement in prayer with us. Many different gifts were used during the course of 25 days at Mercy.

From the parking lot attendants to the servers in the cafeteria, God has a place for all. From the staff that makes sure the surgical instruments are sterile to the anesthesiologist, there was a need for all during our stay. Many different people touched our lives. We have the power to do the same. God has uniquely gifted each of us for a special purpose. *We chose to feel at home at Mercy due to the excellent care.*

HOME AWAY FROM HOME

Jesus felt comfortable in the home of Mary and Martha and their brother Lazarus. They were four friends not just acquaintances. Jesus showed great respect and love for Mary and Martha as well. Are we surprised? They also spoke to Jesus as if He were part of their family. We see in Scripture that Jesus felt their anguish over their brother's death as He was moved to tears before raising Lazarus to life again (verse 33). Was He troubled that they did not believe He could, would, or was He simply showing heartfelt compassion with them?

In the account of Luke we see the closeness revealed between Jesus and this family. Do you have people in your life that you can be close with and share your heart? Do you have a home away from home where you can relax with friends?

"Now it happened as they went that He entered a certain village; and a certain woman named Martha welcomed Him into her house" (Luke 10:38). Jesus was at ease with this family. We can see that their home at Bethany, just outside Jerusalem, was a comfortable place for Jesus and one might consider His home away from home.

Though Jesus felt a deep love for all three, they each had their own personality and different perspectives.

MARTHA'S PERSPECTIVE

When we visit the home of friends and relatives we have a good idea of what to expect. Jesus knew what to expect when he visited with his friends at Bethany. I believe He appreciated the differences among His three friends and also loved them enough to offer constructive advice to their own chosen priorities. This is obvious in Scripture.

Martha's outlook on life was quite different from Mary's. One might say polar opposite. Do you suppose that Martha was a few years older and that just perhaps her age had much to do with her personality and perspective? We find that Martha's words were very practical and efficient. There is absolutely nothing wrong with being practical, using good common sense, and being efficient. As a matter of fact, nothing gets accomplished in life without it at some point. However, if the work that is practical begins to interfere with the more important things in life, we have a problem. God gave us examples in His Word to show us. The Bible says: "Now all these things happened unto them for ensamples: and they were written for our admonition, upon whom the ends of the world are come" (1 Cor. 10:11).

We could probably say Martha was a leader and perhaps even more hospitable than Mary. The Bible says: "Now it happened as they went they He entered a certain village; and a certain woman named Martha welcomed Him into her house" (Luke 10:38).

MARY'S PERSPECTIVE

"And she had a sister called Mary, who also sat at Jesus' feet and heard His word" (verse 39). If you just look at that verse, you might assume that Mary was a lazy sort by leaving the hosting to her sister, but I believe Mary took the position she felt in her heart. While Martha was the host who invited Jesus into the home, Martha chose to be busy while Mary simply sat at Jesus' feet, listening to His every word. I can just imagine she was clinging onto His every word. Don't you? She chose to spend time in His presence rather than running to and fro making sure everything was perfect. Who was the more sociable of the two?

At the heart level, who do you think was more concerned about serving her Lord? Do you think Mary was shy so she didn't greet people at the door? How do you think Jesus would evaluate the scene? He tells us in His Word. The Bible says: "But Martha was distracted with much serving, and she approached Him and said, 'Lord, do You not care that my sister has left me to serve alone? Therefore tell her to help me.' And Jesus answered and said to her, 'Martha, Martha, you are worried about many things. But one thing is needed, and Mary has chosen that good part, which will not be taken away from her' " (Luke 10:40-42).

For us to better understand Mary's actions, let's move to John's account of the same visit.

"Then, six days before the Passover, Jesus [and the disciples] came to Bethany, where Lazarus was who had been dead, whom He had raised from the dead. There they made Him a supper; and Martha served, but Lazarus was one of those who sat at the table with Him. Then Mary took a pound of very costly oil of spikenard, anointed the feet of Jesus, and wipes His feet with her hair. And the house was filled with the fragrance of the oil" (John 12:1-3).

We can see John emphasizes that Mary was humble, convicted and dedicated to her Lord Jesus and His teachings to the point that no expense or personal act was far too great or even demanding for her to honor her Savior. Her attitude, outlook and perspective are what God is looking for in us today. Jesus highly regarded Mary's approach.

We might take note to realize that Martha was so comfortable with Jesus that she voiced her frustration without fear of His response at all. Her words "Do You not care?" and "My sister has left me to serve alone" show her heart and frustration. Martha was obviously close to Jesus to be able to just tell it like she saw it. She didn't even suggest to Jesus that He tell Mary to help her; she told Him very directly.

Martha was consumed by the responsibility of serving a meal. Today, we too, can get so caught up in serving the Lord that we forget the better thing—our ministry to Him by sitting in His presence.

Jesus responded tenderly but also forthrightly to Martha: "Martha, Martha, you are worried and troubled about many things" (Luke 10:41). Martha was stressed out and fretting over what she considered vitally important to her: providing a meal for Jesus and His disciples. One might ask this question, "How important is this in comparison to other priorities?"

"This is why I speak to them in parables: "Though seeing, they do not see; though hearing, they do not hear or understand" ---Matthew 13:13 NIV

HEART CHECK

The heart of our Father God is always turned toward His beloved children. He also speaks to us in many different ways. Have you spent enough time in His Word and learning the ways of the Holy Spirit or do you just know about His creative power?

God wants you to see clearly. Learn to hear His voice and begin to see with His eyes as you spend time studying the Bible, learning from other spiritual leaders, through prophetic words, dreams and visions, and through His still small voice as well as signs.

LORD, teach me the language of love and help me to see through your eyes. Help me to hear and understand so I may serve you well. Amen.

CHAPTER 23

CHOICES

❝ J esus continued: "But one thing is needed, and Mary has chosen that good part, which will not be taken away from her" (Luke 10:42 NKJV). Jesus reveals to us that Mary made a conscious decision to listen to Jesus over preparation of a meal. This might sound lazy or strange to those who think like Martha. It is obvious Martha thought the meal was more important than visiting. I've got news for you today. In families, we have a similar thing going on—adults can be more consumed in what they are receiving, even from parents, than they are in relationship and simply visiting. As with Martha, the most pressing need was preparation of a meal for Jesus and His disciples. Adults might think working harder and longer hours to buy a bigger, better home is a good thing; when all the while they are missing spending time with the family.

Even adult children who have families of their own can lose the best part of relationship with their parents when they view their relationship through eyes of material, natural needs and things, rather than the heart of family. Family is the greatest treasure. What do you suppose is wrong in American families today?

Jesus teaches us that listening to His Word first is of utmost importance. It is not enough just to invite Jesus into the home of your heart; you must also spend time with Him

*through His Word and connecting with other believers in
a church. Martha invited Jesus into her home but failed to
listen to His teaching because she was consumed with cares.*

Mary chose wisely. She chose to listen to Jesus while she
had the opportunity. People make choices and it is all part
of real life. The prophet Moses declared: "I call heaven and
earth as witnesses today against you, that I have set before
you life and death, blessing and cursing; therefore choose
life, that both you and your descendants may live" (Deut.
30:19 NKJV).

Our life is determined by the choices we make every day.
Jesus said Mary had chosen "the good part." What about
you? Have you chosen the "good part?" Jesus tells us our
highest priority in life must be to "seek first the kingdom of
God and His righteousness…"(Matthew 6:33).

JESUS IS WISDOM AND OUR PEACE

Jesus also gives us wisdom: "Man shall not live by bread
alone, but by every word of God" (Luke 4:4). Mary apparently knew in her heart that the words of Jesus were more
important than anything in life, do you? (See Deut. 8:3 and
John 6:63) The words Jesus speaks are spirit and life.

The Word of God was in the presence of Mary, Martha,
Lazarus and the twelve disciples in the person of Jesus
Christ. (See John 1:14-15)

The book of Hebrews reveals the importance of hearing
and taking heed to the Word of God: "Therefore we must
give the more earnest heed to the things we have heard,
lest we drift away. For if the word spoken through angels
proved steadfast, and every transgression and disobedience
received a just reward, how shall we escape if we neglect
so great a salvation, which at the first began to be spoken
by the Lord, and was confirmed to us by those who heard
Him" (Hebrews 2:1-3).

What have you chosen? What did Jesus mean when He spoke of "that good part, which will not be taken away from her?" (Luke 10:42) The apostle John answers the question for us: "All that is in the world—the lust of the flesh, the lust of the eyes, and the pride of life—is not of the Father but is of the world. And the world is passing away, and the lust of it; but he who does the will of God abides forever" (1 John 2:16-17). There won't be any U-hauls in heaven. You won't be taking anything with you except the souls you led to Christ or the ones that were won through a ministry you partnered with in giving.

Compare the word in 2 Peter 3:10-12 as well. "But the day of the Lord will come as a thief in the night; in which the heavens shall pass away with a great noise, and the elements shall melt with fervent heat, the earth also and the works that are therein shall be burned up. Seeing then that all these things shall be dissolved, what manner of persons ought ye to be in all holy conversation and godliness, Looking for and hasting unto the coming of the day of God, wherein the heavens being on fire shall be dissolved, and the elements shall melt with fervent heat?" God's truth and laws will abide forever. I can assure you our bodies won't last forever. They will be replaced with spirit bodies. The spiritual wisdom and knowledge we attain in this life will be ours forever and will never be taken away from us. We must choose not to allow physical needs and wants to consume us.

Like Mary, each of us must learn to live in patient faith. In a world that is lost and filled with the enemy snares, traps, and momentary sensual pleasure, we must choose the part that lasts: "Here is the patience of the saints; here are those who keep the commandments of God and the faith of Jesus" (Rev. 14:12 NKJV).

While the hospital staff was busy with Dan, we trusted God and spent time in the Word. In the Bible, Martha was busy supplying the visitors with things that made them more comfortable while Mary soaked in the words of Jesus like a sponge. Martha was busy with form while Mary concentrated on substance. Jesus commended Mary for choosing the good part, the Word of God, truth and faith of Jesus Christ, which will never be taken away.

As believers, we must choose to follow the example of Mary and desire God's truth above all else. We must also have a Martha to be able to be a Mary. Sometimes we are to be a Martha and other times Mary. Because of our love for God, we will be constrained by His love to see the heart of a matter and do whatever He tells us to do.

Let us think for a moment. When do you suppose one stops serving to truly benefit from listening? You can serve so much that you experience burn out, lose your family, and can become bitter from carrying the so-called load. What would have happened if Dan had waited till *after* tax season? It's pretty obvious. He would have died.

We must choose to balance natural life with our spiritual life. If we choose to spend time with Jesus and submit to His Will, we can accomplish far more in less time. Thank God Dan chose to submit to the plan of God in his life. Thank God he heard the words from Dr. Bower and realized he had only a week to live. We had a struggle with life and death and chose to believe God! He was and is our ONLY hope!

What about the family struggles with blended families who misperceive? What about the blind spots in people's eyes that cause them to assume and misunderstand? How do we handle people and family that attack us when we are choosing to do the right thing in the midst of a chaotic world? What about the "expectant mentality" that is so prevalent in the world today? How do you bring balance in your life and family with struggles?

What about the adult child that has never lived on their own and blows a gasket, spewing venom with their mouth? How do you handle people when they don't respond in wisdom? What causes people to react rather than respond?

On any given day life can seem to be peaceful and the next, someone in the family acts like the devil. I have heard people let words fly that I had never heard before when something happened they didn't expect. How do we have balance with so many different personality types? How do we find peace in the midst of turmoil? How do you stand in a world gone mad?

What happens when our own family doesn't like us? What happens when family puts more emphasis or value on *money and things, rather than relationship?* What happens when you hear a person from your church choir curse and let words fly in the face of adversity? What happens when someone else is driving your car and they get rear-ended at a stoplight? Are you more concerned about stuff than people? What has gone wrong?

What do people who don't know Jesus think when they hear believers acting like the world? What happens to a person's heart when he or she allows the world to damage their soul? God allows things to happen in our lives to reveal what is in our own hearts. God is at work on each of us! No one has arrived to perfection!

If you have experienced any of these, choose to stand with me today on God's Word. He is our very present help in a time of trouble. He is the healer of hearts, not us. He is the one who brings brokenness to the hearts of our teens, our adult children, and our lost family who are bent on going to hell. He is the healer. Our place is to submit to His Word, surrender to His will and guard our own heart above all else.

If you are striving, learn to rest in the power of the Holy Spirit and step into His divine plan for your life, no matter what your personality type. If you will choose to spend time in His presence, read and pray His Word, pray in the Spirit, even your personality can change in His presence.

As we choose to be guided by the Holy Spirit, have our

faith strengthened by Christ, and experience a new intimacy with the Father, you and I can experience release of God's generosity so we can become a hundredfold Christian. The Word of God tells us: "I have come that they may have life, and have it to the full" (John 10:10 NIV).

If we choose to get caught up in personalities, reasoning, and ultimately trying to figure everything out in life, we will be distracted too. A Martha personality is a bottom-line person. They might say, "Get over it" to making you feel like they don't care if you don't respond the same way they do. They are not so emotional when it comes to other people's feelings, but they *are* about their own. They can drop you like a hot potato and send you over the edge *if* you choose to be led by your emotions rather than the Spirit of God.

My husband is a type A personality and much like a Martha. I had to grow up in a whole new dimension when we got married. His personality and the way he reacts actually helped me even get closer to Jesus! I love my husband, but the first love of my life is Jesus. He is the only one who will never leave you nor forsake you. That is why you can't choose to put people on pedestals. You have to find balance.

This week I started to write a note to someone but instead, I chose to simply pray and ask God to move on the person's heart and He did just that. By the very next morning, I had received the answer to the prayer. It was small but I chose to stay out of the way and let God handle it. No, it wasn't in my own home for some of you wondering. It was a matter with a friend.

Some of you reading this now like to figure everything out and try to help God out too. You pray for God to change others, rather than asking God to change you. As individuals, we need to be focused on becoming more like Jesus and trust Him with life.

God is amazing and His ways are always right and true. He knows exactly how to get to the heart of a matter. Ask yourself this question, "How is my heart?" I believe the Church is learning what it means to enter the King's Presence and what it involves. We enter His Presence only through true worship that requires separation from the world.

God allowed Dan to be separated from the world for a few days in such a manner that he actually had no choice but to trust God. It was all in His hands and how thankful I am! Jesus led us right to Mercy Hospital through a series of events.

The Bible tells us that Jesus led Peter, James and John up the mount where they saw him and had a personal encounter. We must choose to come apart as well. If you don't come apart from the world, you will come apart. Everyone needs rest.

We must each have a willingness to deny ourselves and to allow brokenness to be a part of our lives. In the book of Esther, we know Esther allowed herself to be prepared to enter the presence of the king. We must allow the painful processes that come in our lives to prepare our hearts to enter the King's Presence as well.

It is obvious to me the Church is in trial. When King Ahaseurus determined to search for the virgins of the land for a queen to replace the rebellious Vashti, Esther was among the beautiful maidens chosen and brought to the house for preparation. The maidens were placed in the custody of Hegai, the king's eunuch who was the keeper of the women. He gave them the things they needed for purification, a process that is still required today to enter the presence of the King Jesus. Hegai's name means *meditation*. The young women spent much time alone, separated from family, friends, and the things they were accustomed. This was part of their process and so it is again for us today. Don't you know Esther had time to think about everything, including family during her alone time?

Dan had much time to think about what matters in life at Mercy Hospital. He was in God's mercy and grace. God brought him there for "such a time as this" to spare his life.

God brought Esther to the palace and prepared her for the saving of an entire nation.

Esther had been orphaned as a child and when her parents died, Mordecai, her near kinsman, chose to adopt her. Much like Esther and Mordecai, Jesus, our kinsman redeemer has chosen to adopt us into His heavenly kingdom and family. What a privilege. Mordecai is a representation of the Holy Spirit in our lives as well. His watchful eye and nurturing care parallels the relationship of the Holy Spirit.

The sufferings that come into our lives may be caused by physical pain in our bodies to emotional or spiritual distress. Suffering may also come from situations we encounter or people we deal with in life. As we choose to submit to God's plan, our own personal purification processes, there is a balm of Gilead that God begins to pour into our lives. We all have bitter experiences through suffering in life. A chief cosmetic used in preparation in the life of Esther was the oil of myrrh. It is the same for you and I today. It represents the grace for the dealings of God in our lives. We experience brokenness in life that produces tears that make us beautiful in God's eyes. For those difficult times in life, God's grace is sufficient and there is an endless supply.

The Scriptures teach us that a broken and contrite heart God will not despise (Ps. 51:17). *When we suffer, we either are broken and contrite or angry and mad. What is God exposing in your heart today? Do you trust God through the process? Are you able to receive God's blessing and His purification process so the gifts He has placed in your life can be used for His glory?*

When the dealings of God come, it will produce brokenness and tears. Not necessarily for what has happened to you, but you are able to see through His eyes and hear with His heart to understand the real problem at hand. Treatment with the oil of myrrh requires our surrender, obedience and alone time with God. You have most likely tried to resist the purification process at some time in your life.

God will expose and remove anything and everyone that is not going where He has destined you to go. The path God chooses for you will be determined by your willingness to submit to the breaking experiences that come by divine appointment. I believe God sets our days full of divine appointments. We just don't always recognize them. It may be the line in the grocery store that you move from because you are too impatient, only to see the line you moved from clear quickly.

I remember when Dan and I first got married, I observed the funny times he would do this and I knew what was going on but I didn't tell him God was at work in his own life. I just smiled and walked softly. It's funny looking back on it, not because I am making fun of his lack of patience at the time, but the fact I understood and saw what was really happening at the heart level. God had been doing this in my life, not necessarily in the same way, but just the same in different areas. We all struggle in areas and we all have fallen short of the glory of God. No one is perfect. Amen.

The bottom line is that God is purifying our hearts, individually and corporately, so we may be the Church triumphant. I believe there is a place in God that we have not yet experienced. There is much, much more. There is a place even closer—to the heart of the Father. Jesus did not do anything unless He saw the Father doing it.

God is the great heart surgeon and the healer of hearts. He has far greater plans for us than we can realize. He wants us to take *a leap of faith*, believe and spend time in His presence to understand His will.

You and I as individuals nor the Church as a corporate body, cannot know the visitations of God without submitting to the dealings of God that result in brokenness. Whether we are in need of open-heart surgery or emotional surgery from God, He is the great healer to bring us to a place of rest in

Him. Mary at Bethany found this place at the feet of Jesus. Esther went through an entire year of preparation. I don't pretend to know how long the preparation time is in your life, but God does. I don't have all the answers but I know the One who does. His name is Jesus. Say His name now with me, "Jesus, Jesus, the sweetest name I know." He loves us with an everlasting love and is drawing us closer today so we can partner with Him in what He is doing. He wants you to take a leap of faith and believe Him.

Jesus is seated above—at the right hand of the Father. He is praying for us that our faith would not fail. The love relationship is waiting for those who are prepared for it. Obedience is still the key and not being afraid of looking crazy when God gives you an instruction. When we allow the purification process, we are then prepared and constrained by His love to become part of the answer for the deliverance of God's people, His treasure in the earth.

David gives us a beautiful image captured in words on the pages of the Bible. He reveals the bridegroom coming with garments that smell of myrrh, aloes and cassia (Ps. 45:8). He also describes the king's daughter who is glorious within (verse 13). It is only the power of the Holy Spirit operating in our lives that bring change. The inner beauty is wrought by God through the sometimes painful purification processes He ordains to rid us of sinful and selfish ways. Her clothing is of wrought gold and her raiment of fine needlework. The fine needlework represents the intricate workings of God in our life to create a masterpiece. Needles are painful, aren't they? If you and I escape the working of God in our life we will not have His beauty, His character displayed in our own lives. We will miss the entrance into His presence "at such at time as this" for His appointed time.

You don't want to miss God's best in life because of a heart problem. Allow the Holy Spirit to work in your life through the pain you are walking through and choose to surrender to His Will and His ways. His amazing love relationship is waiting for those who are prepared for it. Obedience is the key. If I perish, I perish. I want to please the King and do His work.

"God can do wonders with a broken heart if you give Him all the pieces"
-----*Victor Alfsen*

HEART CHECK

Ask yourself this question:

Have I given my whole heart to the Lord?

CHAPTER 24

COOPERATING WITH THE HOLY SPIRIT

"When you have done the will of God, you will receive what he has promised" (Hebrews 10:36 NIV).

ON DIVINE ASSIGNMENT

It's obvious that God raised Dan up for divine purpose. Let's talk about a very personal and practical way to obtain God's perfect will in your life. Let me ask you a very personal question first and foremost. Do you have a clear objective for your life? Do you have a vision or goal? Would you say you are absolutely positive of God's gift in you and you are living it out or would you say you are drifting through life with no purpose? Are you being tossed about by the winds of habit? Are you tossed about by the winds of fashion in today's world? Are you tossed about by climbing the ladder of your organization or even ministry? Are you tossed about by making sure **your plan** succeeds? Are you tossed about by life's circumstances over which you have no control?

I believe there is nothing more tragic in life than being out of God's will and wandering through life aimlessly. You most likely have talent, special gifts, and abilities but without direction in your life you will end up frustrated, aggravated and bored because you are accomplishing very little. Notice what angers you—for what angers you is sometimes an indicator of where you are anointed to help set others free. What angers you or bothers you the most? What have you walked through in life? What have you learned that can help others? God planned for you and I to have an objective for living. It is provided for us by our faith in Jesus Christ. Did you know that? Let me explain. It is very important whom you follow.

OUR GREAT TEACHER

Who are you following? Who is teaching you? Let's take a look at the book of Hebrews and find out the pattern of Jesus, our greatest teacher: "Therefore, since we are surrounded by such a great cloud of witnesses, let us throw off everything that hinders and the sin that so easily entangles, and let us run with perseverance the race marked out for us. Let us fix our eyes on Jesus, the author and perfecter of our faith, who for the joy set before him endured the cross, scorning its shame, and sat down at the right hand of the throne of God" (Hebrews 12:1-2 NIV).

Let's review the three important truths found here. First, the Christian life is a race that is set up for us in advance. Can you see that? We don't have to map it out because we can see it has already been marked out or mapped out for us. We only have to choose to run the race. It is not a dash or even a sprint, but is much like a marathon like my sister and her husband run quite often. In order to run this type of race, one must throw off everything that hinders or gets in our way. You also need to wear the right kind of clothing and running shoes as well.

I used to run track, races and I also did it in high school as well. The course was always marked out for us. We didn't have to plan it. All marathons are marked out before the day of the race. The runners don't map out the plan. It is already decided for them. The runners simply must decide, commit, train, and show up to run. In this race, perseverance is the key. You must train to endure the long race. It will require patience, endurance and perseverance.

Next, we can see from Scripture, we are to **fix our eyes on Jesus**. He is our inspiration and our teacher. If you choose to take your eyes off Jesus for any length of time, you will ultimately lose your ability to run successfully. You will have lost focus and be encumbered with the cares of the world that weigh you down.

Third, we find that Jesus is *"the author and perfecter of our faith."* Did you catch that wisdom? We don't do it, He does. He is the one who chose us in the first place and He is the one who sets it all on course. We can all see that He is the author of our faith with all the signs, wonders and encouragement He displays in our lives, but we sometimes lose sight of the fact that He is also the perfecter and will bring it to completion. Praise God, right?

Jesus is our pattern. He never starts anything He won't bring to completion. He will never tell you to start something and then tell you not to finish. He never starts anything He is not capable of finishing. That will be great encouragement for many. It is for me! Whatever He has told me to do, He has already equipped me to do and will see me through to the end if I cooperate with Him. I am to partner with Him.

I have a race that is marked out for me by God. I will need endurance for the race that comes from training. Next, I must keep my eyes clearly fixed on Jesus. He is my greatest encourager. He inspires me and He is my teacher and pattern. Third, He is the author and perfecter of my faith. If you will keep your eyes on Jesus, He will not only set you in the race, but will also enable you to keep going and bring you to the finish line victoriously. Isn't that great news?

When we look up to Jesus, just like Jesus did with His Father, we cannot lose the race. The key to His success was His motivation. You and I must enter into His motivation with Him to be successful.

The writer of Hebrews 10:5-10 quotes from Psalm 40 and then applies it to Jesus:

"Therefore, when Christ came into the world, he said: "Sacrifice and offering you did not desire, but a body you prepared for me, with burnt offerings and sin offerings you were not pleased. Then I said, 'Here I am—it is written about me in the scroll—I have come to do your will, O God.'" First he said, "Sacrifices and offerings, burnt offerings and sin offerings you did not desire, nor were you pleased with them" (although the law required them to be made). Then he said, "Here I am, I have come to do your will." He sets aside the first to establish the second. And by that will, we have been made holy through sacrifice of the body of Jesus Christ once for all" (Hebrews 10:5-10 NIV).

God sent His Son Jesus to earth in the form of a man. He gave Jesus a body to sacrifice on our behalf. Jesus came to do His Father's will. This was His ultimate purpose throughout His earthly life—to do His Father's will. He was certain about it and never swayed from His course.

Second, we can see in this Scripture that Jesus played a part according to this Word as well. Look at what the Bible says: "Here I am—it is written about me in the scroll—I have come to do your will, O God." It was written before He came in a scroll. He learned from studying the Scriptures. We are to do the same.

Third, God's purpose and plan in giving Jesus a body was for Him to offer up as the perfect sacrifice on behalf of all mankind. Please note the following three truths: The supreme motivation for Jesus was to do His Father's will. He had a part already written in the scroll of Scripture and God's will actually culminated in the sacrifice of His own body for us.

We have been born to do the Father's will, discover what God says about us in Scripture, and be a living sacrifice daily to God. Jesus is our pattern, our inspiration, and our motivation. He is our reason for living.

HOW WE USE OUR GIFTS WITH THE FATHER

Would you say you are drifting out to sea in the boat of life? Are you controlled by your circumstances and feel like you are being tossed about at sea? Are you controlled by your emotions or circumstances, what you have or don't have in life? Can you imagine how Dan felt when he heard the news about one week left to live? What would you do if you knew you had only one week to live? Who would you go to and make things right? Who comes to mind? What is your objective in life? What is your desire? What is your dream?

You must have a clearly defined objective in life that you pursue steadily on course. One of the greatest benefits of being a Christian is having a clearly defined objective in life—doing the Father's will. God provides each one of us an objective for living. We simply have to choose to study God's word for revelation. Let me explain how the commitment to do God's will was actually worked out in practical ways in the life of Jesus.

I would first like to give you a clue. Be eternity minded in life in all you say and do! I love what the Bible has to say about the journey of Jesus through Samaria and His encounter with the woman at the well. Jesus was simply tired and sat down to rest. The disciples had obviously run out of food, were hungry, and had gone into town to buy some. While Jesus was resting, I love what happened next. He had a beautiful conversation with the woman that came to the well. She got so excited about her encounter that she left her water pot without collecting water and went back into town to tell everyone about this amazing man she met at the well.

Jesus told her about living water for everyone who was thirsty. Jesus remained at the well till His disciples came back and found Him still sitting there resting. Read with me what is in the Scripture next: "Meanwhile his disciples urged him, "Rabbi, eat something." But he said to them, "I have food to eat that you know nothing about." Then his disciples said to each other, "Could someone have brought him food? " "My food," said Jesus, "is to do the will of him who sent me and to finish his work. Do you not say, 'Four months more and then the harvest'? I tell you, open your eyes and look at the fields! They are ripe for harvest. Even now the reaper draws his wages, even now he harvests the crop for eternal life, so that the sower and the reaper may be glad together" (John 4:31-36)

Do you see clearly now? Do you see the precise statement of Jesus? He let us know in Scripture: "My food…is to do the will of Him who sent me." His entire life was based on doing the will of the One who sent Him. Is yours? There are two motivations we find here in the Bible. First, we see the commitment to do the will of God brought forth supernatural, physical restoration in Him. He was strengthened as He did the will of His Father. He was tired and hungry when He came to the well. As He was flowing in the will of His Father with this woman in great need, Jesus was supernaturally strengthened and restored. By sacrificing His own natural needs to do the will of His Father, God restored Him. He sat down as He sensed He needed to go through Samaria.

When His disciples came back with food, Jesus let them know He had already eaten. His disciples did not fully understand the conversation. Jesus explained, "My food…is to do the will of Him who sent me and to finish his work." The disciples looked at the world one way but Jesus looked at the world another. Jesus was already reaping a harvest in that village at that very moment as the woman at the well was sharing her excitement about her encounter with this man Jesus. The disciples were purely seeing life through a natural point of view, but Jesus saw from a spiritual mindset. He was always eternity minded. I have heard people say that you can be so heavenly minded you are no earthly good, but I believe we can be so spiritually minded that we can have and see great earthly good as we step into God's perfect will.

Could this be very similar to what happened at the anointing in Bethany? Could this be what Jesus was referring to when He told Martha she was too busy? Remember what Jesus told Mary? Mary had chosen the good part. Was Mary seeing through the eyes of Jesus and Martha was focused on natural things? Where was their commitment?

Jesus' commitment to do the will of God is what actually gave Him spiritual insight. When you are committed to something, you will choose to see. You will see through the eyes of Jesus and see needs when no one else does. You will hear what people are saying with your heart. Most people live so naturally minded that they miss God's divine interruptions. That is what happened to the disciples that day in Samaria.

DIVINE DISCERNMENT

I know that sometimes I am disappointed in people but I have to say the Lord has always warned me in advance. When we are committed to doing God's will, we will notice everything in life changes. Please look at John chapter 5 with me for a minute. Jesus is discussing the healing of a man who had been paralyzed for many years. Jesus makes an interesting statement in the middle of this discussion: "I can do nothing on My own initiative. As I hear, I judge; and My judgment is just, because I do not seek My own will, but the will of Him who sent Me" (John 5:30 NAS).

When Jesus said, "My judgment is right" what do you suppose He meant? Why did He say this? He tells us... "Because I do not seek My own will, but the will of Him who sent Me." We see a third result of commitment to do the will of God. I believe it is "impartial discernment" or "just judgment." Jesus was never fooled by anyone at any time.

Nobody ever deceived Jesus. He knew Judas was going to betray Him. Jesus saw into the inner motives of all and knew what they were really wanting from Him. Jesus knew exactly how to reach each person, how to touch each person, whether it was a physical or spiritual need all because of His commitment to do His Father's will.

We find a treasure in John 5:30 that we would do well to ponder. How can we avoid being deceived? How can we avoid foolish judgment? How can we appraise a situation and a person accurately? Jesus gave us the answer: "My judgment is just; My discernment is accurate. I see things the way they really are." Why? "Because I do not seek My own will, but the will of Him who sent Me."

There were no clouds blocking the view of Jesus. He was not distracted or clouded in His viewpoint or desire to get His own way. He waited till He heard and saw the revelation of His Father's will, and *then* He made an accurate and just judgment.

Many people lose their focus and get so centered on what *they think* is really happening till they lose spiritual sight into the heart of any matter. They ruin relationships and jump to conclusions without knowing the heart of a person or the accurate findings in any circumstance. They assume and think they know what is going on!

Jesus was tired and hungry when He sat down, but after His encounter with the Samaritan woman, He was restored. So we have it! We see physical restoration in doing the will of God. At Jacob's Well Jesus was tired and hungry, yet in doing the will of God by talking with this woman and sharing the truth with her, Jesus received physical restoration. He wasn't even hungry when His disciples returned with natural food.

Second, Jesus *saw* the harvest field with the eyes of His Father God. His disciples were looking through their natural eyes and therefore, only saw natural needs and the law. Being sold out to Jesus and cooperating with Him with your gifts will give you a totally different viewpoint from others. Your view will differ from the perspective of those around you, just as the disciples' viewpoint differed from Jesus.

Third, Jesus was never fooled by anyone. He was not carried away by wishful thinking, reactions, or emotions. Jesus always waited to hear what His Father was saying. He waited for revelation.

After He exposed Judas, we know what happened. His body was offered up as a sacrifice and the Church began to multiply. We go through the same today. God will expose the spirit of Judas around you and I as well. Even if no one else believes when you hear the Father's warning, God will expose and remove because there is a place He is taking His people that everyone will not choose to go. God is moving the Church from fellowship to Army. God equips and empowers the Church to facilitate the Kingdom of God in the Earth.

MULTIPLICATION – OUTWORKING OF GOD'S WILL

Since wisdom comes from God, let's take a look at a couple other results of how we see the outworking of God's will due to the commitment of Jesus to do the will of God. After Jesus fed the five thousand with five loaves He declared, "I am the bread of life. He who comes to Me shall never hunger, and he who believes in Me shall never thirst. But I said to you that you have seen Me and yet do not believe. All that the Father gives Me will come to Me, and the one who comes to Me I will by no means cast out. For I have come down from heaven, not to do My own will, but the will of Him who sent me. This is the will of the Father who sent Me, that of all He has given Me I should lose nothing, but should raise it up at the last day. And this is the will of Him who sent Me, that everyone who sees the Son and believes in Him may have everlasting life; and I will raise him up at the last day" (John 6:35-40 NKJV).

It is most important to note here what Jesus was saying to us today for our own spiritual application. The Bible is alive and true and still relevant today. There must be a setting aside of our own will before we can do the will of our heavenly Father. Jesus had set his own will aside and refers to "my Father's will" not His own.

I can hardly imagine being one of the disciples and having the amazing opportunity to walk and talk with Him daily. Can you imagine that privilege? Jesus said, "I am the bread of life," and "Everyone who looks to [Me] and believes in [Me] shall have eternal life, and I will raise him up at the last day." What an amazing offer Jesus still gives today. He is the One who can still feed and give life today. He is offering life to this hungry, lost and dying world that is searching and does not understand!

What was the high cost of His anointing? What was the high cost Jesus had to pay? He tells us Himself: "Not doing My will, but the will of Him who sent Me." The world is a busy place with technology on every turn that has the power to keep you focused on your own plans, your own personal agenda, and objectives to the point of death. As long as we are consumed with our own plans, we cannot be operating in divine life. We must choose the will of God rather than our own.

Now think with me for a moment. Jesus was the Son of God and this was true for Him, so wouldn't it be true for you and I as well? Yes, of course! If you and I truly want to be a source of life for all those around us, for the nations and for the broken and hungry world, then we must do the same as Jesus and say, "Not my will but the will of Him who sent me." Will you choose life today? Will you choose to imitate Jesus in the Earth today?

This was also the apostle Paul's own personal testimony in his second letter to the Corinthians: "We always carry around in our body the death of Jesus, so that the life of Jesus may also be revealed in our body. For we who are alive are always being given over to death for Jesus' sake, so that his life may be revealed in our mortal body. So then, death is at work in us, but life is at work in you." (2 Cor. 4:10-12 NIV Holy Bible 1973, 1978, 1984 by the International Bible Society)

As I think back about how death was at work in my own husband, I realize he was positioned by God to do the will of his heavenly Father as well. He prayed to do that so God answered his prayer. While Dan was in Mercy Hospital he was constantly sharing his faith in Jesus with all he met.

Paul explained, "So then, death is at work in us, but life is at work in you." The world needs Jesus. God will allow whatever necessary to cleverly position us to be His ambassadors to the lost and dying around us. If you want to be an ambassador for Christ, death has first to work in you as well. We cannot have life any other way or change the order as we see outlined in Scripture. Pretty obvious, don't you think?

The pattern that Jesus gave us is evidently clear to me. When death is at work in us, then life is at work in others around us. Death was at work in Dan, but God brought His power on the scene and raised Dan up again to live on purpose for His purposes.

The blood of Jesus is our answer. Through the seven places Jesus shed His blood, we have had everything we lost in the Garden of Eden bought back to us.

Jesus took His blood to the Mercy Seat and is seated at the right hand of His Father. He is praying for us that our faith will not fail. Those gone before us are cheering us on.

You and I are not here to do our own will, accomplish our own personal plans, but to do the will of Him who sent us...just like Jesus. God's will is for us to feed and give life to a hungry, lost and dying world. If you will choose to do the will of God and renounce your own plans, I promise you that God will use you in His kingdom purposes. If you will pursue Him with your whole heart with a single-hearted devotion to please the Father, you will find fulfillment in doing the will of God and find yourself being in divine appointments constantly.

This is not possible as long as you are concerned about your own plans, your own agenda, and your own will. You must surrender and be eternity minded. Will you choose life today in imitating Jesus here and now? Will you renounce your own plans and choose to do the will of the One who sent you?

Now, let us take a look at another Scripture found in John 17. The Lord had me studying the book of John a lot when my daddy was sick and in the hospital before God took him home. My greatest desire in life is to please my heavenly Father.

We find another result produced in the life of Jesus by His commitment to please the Father and do His will: "I glorified Thee on the earth, having accomplished the work which Thou has given Me to do" (John 17:4 NAS).

This is the great high-priestly prayer that Jesus offered up to the Father on behalf of His disciples before He was separated from them. Let's take an in-depth look at the word "accomplished." It is a translation of a form of the Greek word, *teleios,* which also means "to finish" or "to complete." Jesus gave us great insight as He constantly talked about doing the will of the Father and finishing it as well. We would do well to remember that and put it into practice.

Jesus told us this after His encounter with the Samaritan woman at the well. Jesus said, "My food is to do the will of Him who sent Me, and to finish His work" (John 4:34 NKJV). Can you see this? Jesus was always moving forward. He was always looking ahead. Jesus is finishing His race. Here He says, "Now I have brought glory to You, O Father, on the earth, because I have come to the end of the work. I have finished it." Doing the will of God always brings Him glory. I can assure you that whatever God has told you to do will bring glory to Him when you do it. One of my favorite passages in Scripture is: "Whatever He says to you, do it" (John 2:5). Nike did not come up with that slogan first.

You might go back to the marathon race I mentioned earlier. Jesus was finishing His race and bringing honor and glory to God. He was finishing well. We must also desire to hear the Father say, "Well done, my faithful servant." I have noticed half-heartedness in people today in some areas of work and service. I was in a store yesterday and a button came off a jacket so I found a clerk and gave it to her so she could properly secure the button for a potential buyer. I noticed she hung the jacket out of place, totally in the wrong section of the store, and put the button in her pocket and went to the back office. She obviously did not care too much about the buyer of the jacket. One could surmise that she was just there to most likely get a paycheck, nothing more. It wasn't about service or even looking ahead.

Lack of service never paints a pretty picture for any organization. Self-seeking service never glorifies God either. When a person's motive for serving God is all about self or promotion, he or she will not bring glory to God. You might notice competition or striving and bickering.

God knows the motive of our heart. There are Christians who are more concerned about their own glory rather than bringing glory to God. They may attract large crowds and have people interested in their productions, but the ultimate end is not really to glorify the Father. In order for us to glorify God, we must first have renounced our own will, and have a single vision for whatever God has assigned us to accomplish in life.

We also need perseverance and a determination not to be moved in the face of opposition. Everyone will not understand where God is sending you or taking you. Check your own heart motive. Will you be able to say like Jesus, "I glorified Thee on the earth, having accomplished the work

which Thou has given Me to do?"
"The race is not to the swift" ---Ecclesiastes 9:11

HEART CHECK

Ask God to keep you in the race and for Him to teach you to love the unlovely. Begin to thank God for leading you to divine appointments on your own course. The Bible says, "But he that endureth to the end shall be saved" (Matt. 10:22 KJV).

CHAPTER 25

IT IS FINISHED AT THE CROSS

As we have viewed the pattern Jesus gave us for life, let us dig a little deeper into the understanding of Scripture: "Then [Jesus] said, "Here I am—it is written about me in the scroll—I have come to do your will, O God" (Hebrews 10:7). We can see the motive of the heart of Jesus was to do His Father's will, right? His course was already marked out and written in the scroll. This is also true for you and me today.

The truths in the Bible are simple. It is really not so complicated. Let's recap on what we have learned thus far: Jesus received physical restoration in a supernatural way when He was about His Father's business. He had a proper view of each situation He encountered that was quite different from those around Him—even His own disciples. Jesus was never deceived as He rendered just judgment. He always saw things exactly how they really were and knew the motive of the hearts of the people. He was a source of life to all around Him and to this world. Jesus glorified God on the earth.

Jesus gave us our job description, if you might say, so we could follow His example to glorify God. We know that God's supreme and highest will for Jesus was the ultimate sacrifice of His body on the cross, right? The Bible says: Therefore, when Christ came into the world, he said: "Sacrifice and offering you did not desire, but a body you prepared for me; with burnt offerings and sin offerings you were not pleased. Then I said, 'Here I am—it is written about me in the scroll—I have come to do your will, O God.'" First he said, "Sacrifices and offerings, burnt offerings and sin offerings you did not desire, nor were you pleased with them" (the law required them to be made). Then he said, "Here I am, I have come to do your will." Jesus sets aside the first to do the second. And by that will, we have been made holy through the sacrifice of the body of Jesus Christ once for all. (Hebrews 10:5-10 NIV)

God prepared a body for Jesus so he could do His will. Jesus sacrificed His own body on behalf of the entire world. It was constantly in the mind of Jesus to finish the work of God and complete God's will. His focus never changed. When you look at the life of Jesus, you can see the emphasis became even stronger nearer the end of His earthly ministry.

The Bible says: "And it came about, when the days were approaching for His ascension [literally, "His 'taking up,'" which refers to Jesus being taken up through His death on the cross], that He resolutely set His face to go to Jerusalem (Luke 9:51 NAS).

We can see by the phrase, "He resolutely set His face" that Jesus knew what was to come. He had already had this conversation with His disciples and told them what was going to happen even though they refused to actually believe Him.

The Spirit of Christ gave the prophet Isaiah the prophetic view of Jesus' life on the earth: "The Sovereign Lord has given me an instructed tongue [a disciple's tongue—Jesus was the disciple of the Father], to know the word that sustains the weary. He wakens me morning by morning, wakens my ear to listen like one being taught" (Isaiah 50:4 NIV).

We must follow this example. Each morning, Jesus spent time in prayer and was constantly in the school of discipleship with His Father. He received directions each day from His Father.

OLIVER

Let me share a sweet story with you. Our neighbor's have a cat named Oliver that we call "Ollie" and he loves treats. Actually, he is quite the spoiled cat now and his owners say he loves us more than them. We started feeding him when he would come to visit. This morning, I was preparing toast with strawberries and mascarpone cheese for breakfast and was making a pot of fresh coffee. I love to smell the aroma of fresh coffee with delightful flavored beans.

This is one of my favorite meals. When I was placing the cheese back in the refrigerator, for some strange reason it fell out of the door and landed upside down on the floor. I picked it up, washed the outside and placed it inside the door again. I felt like someone was watching me. I knew I was the only one up at that moment as Dan had left a little earlier to play golf with a friend. I woke up at 4:30 and got up to write and make an early breakfast.

While I was standing in the kitchen I thought I heard someone crying. Guess who? Oliver was at the back door staring in the window. He was crying for his morning treats. Yes, I opened the door and fed him treats. Oliver loves treats. This is much like we are to be with God. Each morning, we will have a delight in spending time with Him and receiving bread from His table *if* we will first choose to commit to doing so. He will train you. He is the MASTER TRAINER. He is the best teacher. He desires the best for you and me. Don't miss one morsel.

I also realized that God was speaking to me through the cat's name too. I learned the literal meaning for the name "Oliver" is "Olive Tree" in Latin and the suggested character quality is a peaceful heart. The suggested lifetime scripture verse is Philippians 4:7 "So will the peace of God, that surpasses all understanding, keep guard over your hearts and your thoughts in Christ Jesus." I found this in a book on names I have called: What's in a Name? (Compiled by Gayle Palmquist & John Hartzell – pg. 172).

Like Oliver, when we come to the Lord each morning, His peace permeates our heart and soul. That is great news, my friends! We need peace in this world today! The day certainly goes better or either I am better equipped to handle the day after spending time with my heavenly Father.

I mentioned earlier about how when we connect with other people who love God, we can also glean from them and grow in God's Word. Oliver was getting fat from eating at home and eating treats at our home too.

SURRENDER AND SACRIFICE

Let's continue in Isaiah: "The Sovereign Lord has opened my ear, and I have not been rebellious; I have not drawn back. I offered my back to those who beat me, my cheeks to those who pulled out my beard; I did not hide my face from mocking and spitting" (Isaiah 50:5-6 NIV).

Jesus gave Himself over to do the will of the One who sent Him. He gave Himself willing to those who tortured Him. He knew He would not be disgraced. Let's see what the Bible has to say: "Because the Sovereign Lord helps me, I will not be disgraced. Therefore have I set my face like flint, and I know I will not be put to shame" (Isaiah 50:7 NIV).

Jesus knew His course. He knew what He had been sent to do. He knew His purpose to was to do the work God has assigned Him and to finish it as well. God has an assignment for us today. He has a specific assignment for you. He has positioned you to do His will and finish it.

Dan knew God had given him a specific assignment and he wasn't going to give up and give in to bad reports. He chose to trust God and believed Him for divine intervention and healing. God did just that! Dan knew the enemy was trying to cut his life short through sickness.

If Satan doesn't try to cut your life short through sickness and disease, he will use drama, adversity, and trials. In my first book, God's Priceless Treasure, I talk about your assignment and how the devil tries to get you stuck in drama, which is actually the *Devil Racing after My Assignment*. If you have not read that book, get it and read it. You will be greatly encouraged. The enemy wants to get our focus off God and onto our circumstances and struggles. We must purpose in our own heart to set our own face like a flint toward God and do His will. Look to the Father.

Let's continue to the end of the life of Jesus on earth. Jesus had been on the cross for more than three hours and He was close to the end of His life on earth. The Bible says: "Later, knowing that all was now completed, and so that the Scripture would be fulfilled, Jesus said, "I am thirsty." A jar of wine vinegar was there, so they soaked a sponge in it, put the sponge on a stalk of the hyssop plant, and lifted to Jesus' lips. When he had received the drink, Jesus said, "It is finished." With that, he bowed his head and gave up his spirit" (John 19:28-30 NIV).

Jesus did exactly as He had told His own disciples earlier. "Therefore My Father loves me, because I lay down My life that I may take it again. No one takes it from Me, but I lay it down of Myself. I have power to lay it down, and I have power to take it again. This command I have received from My Father" (John 10:17-18 NKJV).

Jesus released His own spirit to the Father (Luke 23:46). One of His last sentences was: "It is finished" (John 19:30). You might ask, "What was finished?" He had finished the will of the One who sent Him. He had finished His assignment! Will you finish your assignment? Will you choose to lay down your own will to do the will of God?

Let's go back again to John: "My food...is to do the will of him who sent me and to finish his work" (John 4:34 NIV). Jesus was victorious in all He said and did. He did everything He was assigned to do and now we have redemption available through His ultimate sacrifice on the cross!

If you take a closer look at the statement of Jesus, "It is finished," you will find in the Greek that it is just one word, *tetelestai*. It means to perfectly complete something. Jesus waited till He had finished His will on earth before He said, "It is finished." He endured pain, shame, rejection and disgrace. I was recently studying the anointing at Bethany and learned something very interesting!

In Mark 14:3, I learned that the oil of spikenard ointment was specifically designed for this "anointing" and was most unusual but necessary in spiritual preparation for Jesus' death and resurrection. The characteristics, usage, manufacturing and purpose of such natural substances often illustrate a divine parallel in the spiritual operation of the Holy Spirit. This extremely expensive ointment, mixed with spikenard, poured out on the feet of Jesus, symbolically represents the costly price He would pay in reviving the honor He laid aside and would then eventually pour out on those who believe Him.

Spikenard is obtained from vegetation growing high in the Himalayas and processed after piercing the bark of the plant with a pointed hook-like instrument. Applied to Jesus' feet, soon to be pierced by the nails on the cross, this ointment prophetically demonstrated the pathway Jesus would walk upon to receive the honor due Him. (Note on Mark 14:3 The Revival Study Bible, pg. 1385 NKJV).

You can see more clearly now how God uses things in the natural to give us revelation in the spirit realm. I don't believe it was the nails that actually held Jesus to the cross. I believe it was the Father's great love and the perfect will for Jesus, His Only Begotten Son. What a sacrifice for you and me!

WILL YOU FOLLOW?

Will you follow the example of Jesus and use your gifts to do the will of the Father? Will you allow the Holy Spirit to equip and inspire you to finish well? Will you choose to die to your own will to take up the will of God? Based on how the Lord has taught me, I can share what I have learned from God and studying His word. Our first step is to choose to do the will of God. The apostle John recorded that Jesus said: "If anyone chooses to do God's will, he will find out whether my teaching comes from God or whether I speak on my own" (John 7:17 NIV).

Let's check out the Greek word that is translated here as "chooses." It is actually a form of the verb, *theleo,* which means "to will" or "to determine." I believe many people underestimate the power of God and His power to speak today. I also believe many people underestimate the power of their own will in their lives. I have seen many people choose to go down a wrong path or take a wrong direction in life, even after hearing warnings from God. They later end up in a mess and have years to deal with the problems they could have avoided *if only* they had listened *and obeyed* the warnings. *However, if you choose to turn to God **He can take your mess and give you a message that brings hope to other people.***

I often wonder what on earth would cause a person to hear many warnings and directions and still choose their own way. It doesn't make good sense to me. God knows everything. He knows all the details. His way is always the best, so what in mankind is so bent on doing things his own way? It is the will, my friend.

I can assure you that if you don't choose God's will you will not finish well. Jesus sets before us life or death. We have a challenge to face. Will you choose to do the will of God or your own?

We all have a will and we all have a decision to make. Make it a point today to choose to do God's will. Jesus told us, "If anyone chooses to do God's will, [then] he will find out whether my teaching comes from God."

If you are a person who wants an outline for the rest of your life, you will have a problem. Many want God to show them the entire plan, perfectly laid out with detailed instructions for the rest of their life or they won't budge. This is not how it works. You must first choose to do God's will and *then* He will lead you.

Let me explain a little further. If you are married, you have chosen to be committed to your spouse, right? This commitment leads to understanding if you truly desire to have successful relationship, correct? You first choose to commit and then you find understanding. *When we choose to commit to the will of our Heavenly Father, then He begins to unfold our God-given destiny and instructions.* It comes step by step.

The word "if" is not a decision. You will have to choose. Don't waste your life in neutral.

The next step is the sacrifice of your own life or body. The Bible clearly tells us we have to sacrifice our bodies to do the will of God as well. Paul tells us: "There, I urge you, brothers, in view of God's mercy, to offer your bodies as living sacrifices, holy and pleasing to God—this is your spiritual act of worship" (Romans 12:1 NIV).

God wants us to make ourselves available to Him for His kingdom purposes in the earth. When you offer your body to God, you no longer decide where to go or even what to eat. You have given up the right to make those decisions. Whatever we commit to God, He takes care of just like we experienced in Mercy Hospital. God supernaturally intervened on every turn for the saving of Dan's life. God goes to extreme measures for the saving of lives, both physically and spiritually. Whatever is placed on the altar of God belongs to God.

Let me tell you what God has in mind. I love this verse: "For I know the plans that I have for you," declares the LORD, "plans for welfare and not for calamity to give you a future and a hope" (Jer. 29:11 NAS).

God has a great plan for your life but you must first commit it to Him. After this, you will be given understanding. It is a step-by-step process. After we offer our bodies, yes you guessed it; we must renew our minds through the Word of God. Paul tells us emphatically: "Do not conform any longer to the pattern of this world, but be transformed by the renewing of your mind. Then you will be able to test and approve what God's will is—his good, pleasing and perfect will" (Romans 12:2 NIV).

Once you decide to do anything, something happens in your mind. Much like starting to walk, the brain sends a signal to move your legs and feet. The active decision causes you to no longer think like the world thinks. You begin to think like God.

You and I both know that worldly people are just flat out selfish. You can be in a conversation and be nearly blown out of the water with the words that come out of a person's mouth, right? Don't you ever wonder what on earth some people are thinking? If you are a worldly person, your first question will be: "What's in it for me" or "How will this turn out for me?" The person with a renewed mind centers on God and around God. He or she thinks, "Will this glorify God" and "Is this God's will for my life?"

Thank God my husband had spent much time with the Lord so He could be content even in his suffering as he waited, having two open-heart surgeries, two mini-strokes, and having to rebuild his strength by walking with his hospital pole, back and forth, down the halls. Thank God he was able to take a leap of faith and believe God for his total healing. This is what happens to us when we spend time in the presence of God.

You must continue your relationship through abiding in His Word daily. Dan had renewed his mind before the storm. Storms will come in life.

When you renew your mind, you will find out the will

of God. God will not give you revelation until you have first made the commitment. The actual commitment brings release in your mind for renewal. The mind is quite fascinating to me, but that's another book in entirety. When your mind is renewed, you will be able to discern the will of God and His plan for your life.

You will most likely find out that God's plan is quite different than you might think. Satan will attack you and use people also to do the same. He will whisper in your ear that doing God's will is hard and that you won't make it. He will make you think you are going crazy and tempt you to throw in your towel to give up.

Instead of throwing in your towel, be like Jesus and pick up your towel to help others with their walk—like He did! He bent down and washed the feet of the disciples. They did not understand. They too, had to become servants.

Actually, doing God's will is the most fulfilling life! You will wonder how on earth you lived before, once you move forward in God's plan for your life. It is exciting but there can be pain as well. You must surrender. Let me recap again so you have it clearly in view:

Supernatural restoration and refreshing

Just like Jesus experienced at Jacob's Well, you will find refreshing and supernatural, physical restoration. Jesus was not limited and you won't be either, as long as you depend on the Holy Spirit's operation in your life.

A Seer – Proper view the way God sees

Jesus saw things the way they really were with clear vision. When you are committed to doing God's will, you will see clearly too!

Just judgment and discernment

Jesus was not deceived nor was he fooled. He saw the real intent and motive of the heart of all people. He had just judgment and discerned clearly. So will you!

A vessel of life to others

Jesus gave life to those He encountered and so will you. You and I will be used by God to be streams of life supernaturally to those around us when we learn to flow by His Spirit and are committed to doing His will.

DEEP PEACE AND PERSONAL FULFILLMENT IN DOING GOD'S WILL

Jesus said, "I have glorified You on the earth. I have finished the work which You have given Me to do" (John 17:4 NKJV). *IF we will commit ourselves to God, surrender to His will and to finishing well with our whole heart, we, too, will be able to glorify the Lord with our assignment.*

Our personal commitment to doing God's Will brings heaven to Earth. The actual commitment to do His Father's will was the motivation that brought Jesus from heaven to earth in the form of a baby. He grew through the things He suffered to be obedient to the finish.

"When you have done the will of God, you will receive what he has promised" (Hebrews 10:36).

We are called by God to love Him, love people and pass it on. Will you? Will you surrender fully today, if you haven't already? What is holding you back?

You will find deep peace and personal fulfillment in your soul if you will totally surrender your will to His will as you surrender your own claim of self-control. You will discover a new sense of destiny and a new sense of purpose as God reveals His perfect will in your life. What are you waiting for? Choose today. Decide. Don't waste another day! You can receive supernatural restoration, receive God's promised rewards, live free from deception, be a life giver to all those around you, and find deep peace and personal fulfillment in glorifying God through your assignment on earth. Won't you make the decision today?

"When you have done the will of God, you will receive what he has promised" (Hebrews 10:36 NIV). Remember, if you aim at nothing, you will be sure to hit it. You can miss what God has planned for you *if* you don't make a choice. *Take a leap of faith and dare to believe God!*

"When I was a child, I talked like a child, I thought like a child, I reasoned like a child. When I became a man, I put childish ways behind me" — 1 Corinthians 13:11 NIV

HEART CHECK

Ask yourself these questions:

Will I purpose in my heart to follow after Jesus and surrender to His will and ways?

The best way to know God is through His Word. To cultivate a heart of communication, you simply choose to get up each morning and spend time reading the Bible, in prayer and listening. Ask God to show you a hurting world through His eyes.

Am I basing my relationship with Jesus on my church affiliation, traditions or my own good deeds instead of the finished work of the cross?

Do I have deep peace in my life?

Ask God to show you the areas where you have not surrendered. You will begin to recognize peace where you have surrendered. You will feel anxiety in the places you have not fully surrendered to God.

CHAPTER 26

LISTEN, OBEY, COMMIT AND LEAVE A LEGACY

"Therefore this generation will be held responsible."
—Luke 11:50

I firmly believe when we choose to listen and really hear what the Lord is saying, we will hear Him. I also believe when we purpose in our heart to seek God and look for Him, we will see Him. When we say, "Morning by morning new mercies I see," we will see, perceive and understand in far greater measure. Only those who purpose in their heart to hear and obey actually do so. Perception and understanding come primarily through hearing the voice of God. Once we have learned to hear the voice of God, we begin to see and truly become a Seer. We will see His goodness on every turn. The goodness of God is the foundation of a Seer's call. Paul understood this great foundational truth and knew that the love of God truly never fails. He had personally experienced the love of God. I have personally experienced the love of God and continue to do so.

The disciple whom Jesus loved, wrote, 'God is Love," and was able to see the end time Revelation of God because he was rooted in the love of God and His goodness. God desires that we know His love and exhibit it as well. This is our ultimate purpose in the earth…to know God and make Him known.

When we spend time praying in the Spirit, we are changed. When we interpret by the Spirit of God, then and only then will we be able to comprehend the greatness of God. You will see things you've never seen before. There is always more in God. The Bible is a true and relevant up-to-date book. We find hope in God's Word. The Word of God is alive.

Keep praying in the Spirit. God will always be close. You will be able to see more and hear better as you spend time in His presence. He is the very air you and I breathe. Seek Him with your whole heart and believe Him for miracles in your life as He has shown in our lives. Thank God for raising my husband up from early death and for giving him a new lease on life to share his faith to the next generation.

YOU DON'T KNOW WHAT YOU DON'T KNOW

I firmly believe that understanding the things of God is vital to walking in the fullness of what God has for you and me. God gave us this privilege through the New Covenant in Jesus Christ. I don't claim to know everything nor have I arrived to the fullness but I do know I have access to my Father in heaven and so do you.

You don't know what you don't know till you meet someone who knows something you don't. There is always more in God. His ways are higher than our ways and He speaks to us throughout the day. There is always more to be seen in God!

I woke up a few nights ago and each time I woke up the clock said 4:47 AM. I woke up three times so I knew this was significant. I don't believe the church body has good understanding of the portals or access we have to God through prayer. Probably most don't even know of their existence or even their significance.

The world is fixated on the supernatural but it seems the church is sometimes afraid of the Spirit of God and how

He chooses to speak to us. He still speaks and still divinely intervenes. God wants us to take a *leap of faith* and dare to believe Him. It is time to believe Him at His every Word! I sensed the Lord was speaking to me about 4:47 so I looked up John 4:47. The Bible says, "When he heard that Jesus had come out of Judea into Galilee, he went to Him and implored Him to *come down* and heal his son, for he was at the point of death" (John 4:47 NKJV).

In John 4:46-54 we can see that the healing of the nobleman's son not only demonstrates Jesus' power to heal, but it also underscores the principle that He did not regard signs and wonders as ends in themselves. Rather, they were at the very least intended to bring the recipients of the miracle to faith in Jesus Christ.

I believe we are still called to pray or implore God to *come down* to heal today. When we pray and earnestly seek God with our whole heart, I believe He brings Heaven to earth for those that love Him. I believe this is what happened to Dan at Mercy Hospital.

I had to choose on purpose to commit the entire situation to God, for He was the only one that could fix the problems. I lifted up my eyes toward the Lord in prayer and told the Lord I chose to commit Dan and this entire heart issue to Him. (See Matthew 17 and see how the disciples lifted up their eyes and saw no one but Jesus only. He touched them when He saw they were afraid).

After driving out of Mercy Hospital and seeing the stop sign at the corner of Randolph Road with the sticker reading: WORRYING underneath the STOP, I knew God Himself was saying, "Stop worrying" to me. Worry is sin and should not even be in our vocabulary as Christians.

Do you worry? Do you know how to cast your care upon the Lord because He cares for you? Take time to study this out in Scripture. Ask the Lord to forgive you for worrying and begin to say what He says about you and your situation.

Melanie, a dear friend of ours, was also at the hospital this day and as she was driving to pick up her kids she was praying to God to let her know He heard her prayers for my husband Dan. She saw a sign that said—love to Dan (LOVE2DAN)... and knew that only God could have orchestrated that confirmation. God goes to extreme measures to encourage us to keep our trust in Him for the answer.

Let's take a look at Scripture for a moment. The Bible says, "Lift up your head, O gates, And be lifted up, O ancient doors, That the King of glory may come in" (Psalm 24:7). You might be asking, "Why talk about portals?" What are ancient doors and gates? These are portals of access established by God from the third heaven to earth. I believe this is part of what happened while we were at Mercy Hospital. I believe the dream the Lord gave me warning about the plexi-glass machine with the light purple fountain or stream of liquid flowing from me all the way through the heavens to the Mercy Seat was very significant and God showed it to me *on purpose*.

God was showing me things to come and that He was bringing Heaven to earth at Mercy. God brought Heaven to earth and His power manifested at Mercy in my precious husband's life. He had committed his whole life to God many years earlier but had recently been emphasizing his desire to do full-time ministry with me in the future, so God was at work behind the scenes making every crooked place straight. The enemy was opposing and trying to cut my husband's life short, but God brought miracles and divine intervention on the scene. (See Scriptures: Isaiah 45:2, Luke 3:5)

We also learned the enemy was operating through people against one of our businesses to attack our finances. God exposes all hidden truth and He sees every detail. The Lord gave me an interesting Scripture for this situation. "Give us help from trouble, for the help of man is useless. Through God we will do valiantly, for *it is* He *who* shall tread down our enemies" (Psalm 60:11-12 NKJV Nelson). We began to pray these verses back to God in prayer.

We can read about Daniel praying in Daniel chapter 10, verse 13, and how the prince of the kingdom of Persia was standing in opposition to the angel sent in response to Daniel's prayers. Portals are unobstructed by demonic access so that the angels may travel from heaven and back so that provision may be delivered, transportation, translation, and revelation are given to men and women. Could this be what happened at Mercy and the reason we were there for 25 days? Could it be there was major warfare in the heavens blocking the answer much like what happened to Daniel in the Bible? Do we give up too easily when it comes to prayer and waiting for the answer? Do you?

We know from Scripture that Michael, one of the chief princes (angels) came to help fight through the portal in the demonic land of Babylon to give Daniel understanding. Thank God that Daniel didn't give up in praying before the end of his 21st day. Can you imagine what would have happened if he had given up on day 19?

ANOTHER PORTAL IN THE LIFE OF JACOB

Jacob had a dream that is recorded in the book of Genesis. Let's read, "He had a dream, and behold, a ladder was set on the earth with its top reaching to heaven; and behold, the angels of God were *ascending* and *descending* on it" (Genesis 28:12). God is standing at the top of the ladder in verse 13. "And behold, the LORD stood above it and said, "I am the LORD, the God your father Abraham and the God of Isaac; the land on which you lie, I will give it to you and to your descendants."

God reveals a portal to Jacob in a dream to show Jacob's destiny to him. I remember being in a church service when we first moved to Charlotte and a lady came up to me to share a word of prophecy. She said an elder in the church saw me in a ladder like Jacob's ladder with angels ascending and descending and he saw my face in the ladder in pain. I will never forget what he told her to tell me. He said, "The Lord says don't ever allow anyone to pull you out of your walk with God, not even those who purport to be Christians." What a word!

As I reflect over my life, I now have greater understanding of what God was revealing. He shows us things in part. I stand amazed at God and His extravagant love for us! Don't you?

I remember the Lord making me wonder about the word *ESCADA* just after this happened, so I was determined to find understanding. I learned it was Spanish and when translated into English meant ladder or stairs. It also means stairs, stair, or ladder in Portuguese. It can also mean escalator.

The company Escada was founded by a beautiful Swedish woman named Margaretha Ley. There was also an Irish thoroughbred named Escada. Margaretha and Wolfgang Ley met with adversity when the important fashion fairs refused to grant them space. Unwilling to accept defeat, the Leys named the collection Escada after an Irish thoroughbred racehorse. It is an amazing story of how her husband packed a Volkswagen bus with samples, traveling throughout Europe in search of clients and retail outlets.

Escada broke fast at the starting gate and sales skyrocketed, beating all odds. Wolfgang Ley took on the roles of salesman, financier and production and marketing director. His wife Margaretha, a former model for French couturier Jacques Fath, developed the fashion concept. In 1986, Escada went public on the Frankfurt and Munich exchanges. After the death of Margaretha in 1992, the Escada design team continued her legacy.

Today, Escada, still based in Munich with a wholly owned fragrance company in Paris, has 1,300 employees and owns all of its manufacturing facilities. The company has subsidiaries in the United States, Canada, Britain, Italy, France, Spain, Japan and Asia. (http://www.afeyewear.com/include/library/escada_eyewear.aspx)

This is a natural story of how two people never gave up. Whether you own a business or have a ministry facing adversity, God still has a great plan for you. If you have received a bad medical report, God still has the final word! He has nations for you to impact. He has great plans for you. He will open the windows of Heaven to bless you when you seek Him and do His will.

Dan and I never gave up at Mercy. God intervened and Dan is still alive. If God will do it for us, He will do it for you. God had a plan for the owners of Escada Corporation. He has a plan for you.

I don't know if these people were believers or not, but I do know they chose to operate in God's principles of success. They named their business after a racehorse that was a winner. We have the name above all names and His name is Jesus. He has great things prepared in advance for us to do. People of all nations have adversity, both in business and in their personal lives. God cares about all the details.

Much like my determination to understand the word ESCADA, God put a determination in me to understand why people do the things they do. I asked God for wisdom to help His people and He began to teach me Himself.

OPEN HEAVENS

Once in praise and worship at our local church, the Lord opened the heavens and showed me my daddy and the Lord standing over the gates of heaven smiling down at me. I could feel the tears of joy streaming down my face. What a vision of hope that my heavenly Father allowed me to see. This was a gate or ancient door that opened up for me. He has allowed me to see my daddy a few times in this manner. I believe God opens the heavens to what our natural eyes can't see, but our spiritual eyes can.

God knows we are frail. He knows we are weak and have problems but loves us anyway. Aren't you glad? I know I am. I am thankful He is all I need and He is the "Great I AM!"

Sometimes you have to leave where you are to go where God sends you to hear Him. The wind of the Spirit blows where it will. We can see in the Bible that God established a portal from the third heaven to Mt. Horeb. Elijah was instructed to leave from sitting under a juniper tree to Mt. Horeb to *see* and *hear* what God had to show him. You might remember that wise men travel to see God. The Three Wise Men came searching for Jesus.

"So He said, 'Go forth and stand on the mountain before the LORD.' And behold, the LORD was passing by! And a great and strong wind was rending the mountains and breaking in piece the rocks before the LORD; {but} the LORD {was} not in the wind. And after the wind an earthquake, {but} the LORD {was} not in the earthquake" (1 Kings 19:11 NASB).

We also learn that the person who sits, waits and listens at the Lord's gate will be blessed. (See Proverbs 8:34) Let's also take a deeper look in the book of Isaiah. The Bible says, "Oh, that You would rend the heavens {and} come down, That the mountains might quake at Your presence--As fire kindles the brushwood, {as} fire causes water to boil--To make Your name known to Your adversaries, {That} the nations may tremble at Your presence! When You did awesome things which we did not expect, You came down, the mountains quaked at Your presence" (Isaiah 64:1-3 NASB Emphasis).

The Bible tells us that the man who listens to Him, watching daily at His gates and waiting at His doorposts will be blessed. Be honest with God in prayer. Tell him how you are, how you feel and ask for His help. Pretending is a snare. Real life happens to real people. People get into trouble. Don't wear a mask and cover your pain. Beneath lies the real you in confusion, in aloneness, and in fear. God wants you to know He hears and answers prayer. He changed the Samaritan woman by one encounter at the well. He can change you.

If we show weakness, meet with failure, or fall into sin, we must realize that our position in Christ is what makes us acceptable to God and not our behavior. Be totally honest with God. When God sends people to help you, be honest with them and learn to accept them as God's representatives. Find someone you can trust and share your heart. Seek counsel and ask God for wisdom.

ANGELIC HELP THROUGH PORTALS

Let's take a look at the life of Lot. In Genesis 19:1 we find that Lot is waiting at the gate of Sodom when two angels appear to him. The gate of the city was not only an outlet but was also where meetings of great nature were held in the ancient world.

The Bible says, "And there came two angels to Sodom at even; and Lot sat in the gate of Sodom: and Lot seeing [them] rose up to meet them; and he bowed himself with his face toward the ground."

The Lord states He will go down to investigate, spy out, or scout out for Himself to see the evil that is bringing a stench into the heavens. "I will *go down* now, and see whether they have done altogether according to the cry of it, which is come unto me; and if not, I will know" (Gen. 18:21 ESV).

It seems clear to me that the "go down" happens when the angels appear at the gate or ancient door of the city. Can you see that?

We see **portals of provision** where God opened the doors of heaven and fed the Hebrews in the desert the manna or food of angels in Psalm 78:23-25. I saw God send angels of mercy to bring His provision to pass for my precious husband at Mercy. Thank God for His help! See Psalm 103:20.

The Bible says, "Though He had commanded the clouds from above, and opened the doors of heaven, and had rained down manna upon them to eat, and had given them of the corn of heaven, man did eat angels' food: He sent them meat to the full" (Ps. 78:23-25 KJV). I believe God is sending spiritual rain that refreshes and restores us today. He wants to send it on us individually and as a nation. When He reigns over our lives, we reign with Him in the supernatural realm.

Ezekiel – Portals Opened

Let's look at another place in the Word of God where portals opened. "Now it came to pass in the thirtieth year, in the fourth month, in the fifth day of the month, as I was among the captives by the river of Chebar, that the heavens were opened, and I saw visions of God" (Ezekiel 1:1 KJV). "And the hand of the LORD was there upon me, and He said unto me, "Arise, go forth into the plain, and I will there talk with thee. Then I arose, and went forth into the plain; and, behold, the glory of the LORD stood there, as the glory which I saw by the river of Chebar: and I fell on my face" (Ezekiel 3:22-23 KJV). Again we see in Scripture: "And it came to pass in the sixth year, in the sixth month, in the fifth day of the month, as I sat in mine house, and the elders of Judah sat before me, that the hand of the Lord GOD fell there upon me. Then I beheld, and lo a likeness as the appearance of fire: from the appearance of his loins even downward, fire; and from his loins even upward, as the appearance of brightness, as the color of amber" (Ezekiel 8:1-2 KJV). The color of amber is like glowing metal.

Are you getting excited like me? God has much more for us as we seek Him. God wants to bring His resurrection power to what appears to be dead in your life. He did it for Dan. He wants to bring healing to your heart. He wants to do heart surgery on the places where you have allowed the enemy to make it hard and stony. He wants you to have faith again, to dare to believe Him at His very WORD! God wants to change us as we spend time in His presence so we will shine His light to others, even when they don't want to see or hear.

PORTALS OVER NATIONS/GEOGRAPHICAL LOCATIONS

Habakkuk

Often God will establish a portal over a certain nation or geographical location after a faithful servant, or group of servants, have spent much time in prayer and supplication. In the second chapter of Habakkuk we find the prophet faithful to *watch and see* what the Lord will say to him and to write it down. Habakkuk is waiting at the place he has established to faithfully pray and wait upon the Lord. *Have you established a place of prayer where you wait upon the Lord? If not, I would encourage you to do so today. There is no time like the present.*

The Bible says, "I will stand upon my watch, and set me upon the tower, and will watch to see what he will say unto me, and what I shall answer when I am reproved. And the LORD answered to me, and said, Write the vision, and make [it] plain upon tables, that he may run that readeth it" (Hab. 2:1-2 KJV). God still gives instructions today.

DIVINE CONNECTIONS ON AN ESCALATOR

I remember hearing the Lord speak to me to take my mother and go to a conference in Upper Marlboro, Maryland called "Unstopping the Wells" many years ago. We obeyed and went. We met lots of amazing people and had the opportunity to meet Dr. Don and Mary Colbert on this trip. He was actually speaking at the conference.

I also met a lady on an escalator one evening when we went to dinner. I spoke to her and we struck up a conversation. Imagine that! We are still friends today. She and her husband live in Texas now but we have remained friends and have stayed connected through tough times and good times.

God positioned her mother-in-law here at CMC Main Hospital in Charlotte so Mother and I could visit and pray with her while she was there. God positions us in life as we simply go about doing natural things. That is how it all works together. He knows how to connect us with others for His purposes.

I remember being in an airport after speaking at a women's conference in the New York area and having a strange thought about my friend. I sent her a text to share what the Lord had spoken to my heart as I sat having a cup of warm soup while waiting in the airport. To my surprise, she responded immediately. I hadn't spoken to her in months, but in one moment, God gave me a word for her that brought great encouragement as she was walking through a tough time. I had no idea, but God did! That again, is the love of God and how He operates. Only God can get the credit. We are just the vessels He flows through to bring about His purpose.

Just like angels are ascending and descending from heaven, God is arranging meetings on escalators. He divinely connects for His purposes that might not be fully revealed for years to come. God knows how to connect us with the right people.

HEART CHECK

Ask yourself these questions:

Who has God been trying to connect me with that I have ignored?

What am I doing to leave a legacy?

How can I learn to seek God?

When called on to defend your faith in God, don't become defensive. View every moment as a teaching or learning opportunity. Any defense you might think of on your own can be challenged in the natural. The supernatural words given to you by God's Spirit will silence all human reasoning and critics. Let the Spirit of God be your defense. God connects us with people on purpose.

"And when you are brought to trial in the synagogues and before rulers and authorities, don't worry about what to say in your defense, for the Holy Spirit will teach you what needs to be said even as you are standing there" —Luke 12:11-12 NLT

CHAPTER 27

LIVING SUPERNATURALLY
IN THE NATURAL

Y ou can see through the accounts in this book that we can learn to walk in the supernatural *in the natural* when God fills our well. Much like the Samaritan woman who came at noon to fill her water jar, she was barren and empty inside. She was apparently ashamed to come when others would come to draw water. God wants us to come to Him with all our past hurts, our pain, brokenness, and lay our lives down to pick up His will. His will is living in His perfect plan for our lives.

The Samaritan woman was so overwhelmed and filled by one encounter with Jesus that she left her jar (which represented her empty past) and went back into the village to share about this encounter. Her testimony brought change and an entire harvest for that village. Her story brought the people to Jesus Himself. That's the way it still works, my friends. He wants to unstop your well and fill you with the river of life that never runs dry.

You have to move when the LORD says move. You must learn to watch for Him. He calls you friend. He was watching over Dan at the hospital. He heard my heart cries for His help.

The Lord has promised us, that as long as we remain at our current location, the portal will be established. We must obey God and stay divinely connected with Him and the place He positions us. When we obey God we live in divine connection. When we leave the house the portal will be removed as well.

My life also changed drastically after my first trip to Israel. I know that like myself, many Christians, who travel to Jerusalem also report receiving divine revelation of the things of God through supernatural experiences such as dreams, visions, transportations back and forward in time. These are not uncommon but common in Christians who are totally committed to Jesus and seek to hear Him. I believe God has established portals over Jerusalem as well. God is not telling us to seek portals but to seek Him so we can draw closer and hear His instructions.

When I was staying in a room at a hotel in the middle of the city of Jerusalem, I remember having a dream there were lions outside the window. I woke up and shut the windows. The lion may symbolize God as a lion sleeps with its eyes open, God never slumbers nor sleeps as He watches over His children.

GOD'S PORTALS OVER PEOPLE

I also believe God establishes portals over people as He did with Jesus. I believe God still gives revelation and reveals mysteries. The Bible says, "And He said to him, "Truly, truly, I say to you, you will see the heavens opened and the angels of God ascending and descending on the Son of Man" (See John 1:51).

"Now when all the people were baptized, it came to pass, that Jesus also being baptized, and praying, the heaven was opened" (Luke 3:21 KJV).

"While he was still speaking, a bright cloud overshadowed them, and behold, a voice out of the cloud said, 'This is My beloved Son, with whom I am well-pleased; listen to Him!" (See Matthew 17:5).

"After being baptized, Jesus came up immediately from the water; and behold, the heavens were opened, and he saw the Spirit of God descending as a dove {and} lighting on Him, and behold, a voice out of the heavens said, "This is My beloved Son, in whom I am well-pleased" (See Matthew 3:16-17).

When we seek God, He will let us know He is pleased with us, and show Himself strong on our behalf. That is the love of God, my friends. His love is truly amazing. (Read my first book: GOD'S PRICELESS TREASURE for more amazing stories)

I remember a few years ago, the Lord gave me a dream where I saw myself sitting with the Apostle John on the isle of Patmos. While John was on the isle of Patmos, a portal opened where he began to receive great revelation of things to come.

I also remember being on a trip to Israel and the Lord allowed me to see the word SOPHIA on the terminal gate flashing. I thought that I must be at the wrong terminal gate but realized everyone else was there from our church that was going on the trip. It was quite interesting. I went to the gate to check to make sure I was still at the right place. How many of you know it is good to ask questions to make sure you are at the right place?

When the door was opened to the jet way, we all began to walk to our appointed seats. The Holy Spirit whispered a Scripture to me and I sat there and read it immediately. "In whom are hid all the treasures of wisdom and knowledge" (Col. 2:3 KJV Cambridge Ed.) As I began to study the Hebrew/Greek I saw the word *"sophia."*

I knew the Lord Himself was showing me that He was going to give me His wisdom through the terminal gate flashing. He was opening a new gate to me for His hidden wisdom and mysteries.

I remember on another occasion Dan and I were on a flight about to leave Nevada. We were sitting in our seats and waiting for the flight to prepare for departure. I was reading my Bible and writing in my journal. I heard the Lord say ever so softly, "If this plane takes off, it will crash." I wrote this down and began to ask God to block the plane from even departing if that was Him warning me. A few minutes later, the pilot announced we had a mechanical and they were trying to fix the problem. I showed Dan my notes in my journal at that point and what I had written about the warning from God in His sweet voice.

After about ten more minutes the captain announced the plane was grounded due to right engine failure and we would be de-boarding the flight to board another plane for Charlotte. I also prayed that God would get us home no matter what. It was kind of strange because the airlines put all the passengers on our flight on another plane that was already scheduled and de-boarded those passengers for a later flight. They failed to realize there was a race being held in Charlotte at the time and hotels were booked. Needless to say, God answered our prayers and saved us from calamity.

I would imagine there are many, many times when we are unaware of God's divine intervention. I thank God for His training in my life so I would know to recognize Him and move into action when He speaks. God goes to extreme measures for the saving of lives; physically, spiritually and financially.

He trains our hands to war. He trains us for the battle in life, not against people, but against the enemy. He trains us to be Generals in the Army of God so that we hear Him at the slightest whisper at the door of heart to move into action. Choose today to find out God's plan for your life. His Will for your life is His Word! He has great things prepared in advance for you and I to accomplish through His power.

Take time to read the Bible. Take time to connect with God, for He cares for you. He wants you to learn to hear and recognize His voice so you can obey Him quickly. Let's take a look right now: "After these things I looked, and behold, a *door* [standing} open in heaven, and the first voice which I had heard, {the sound} of a trumpet speaking with me, said, 'Come up here, and I will show you what must take place after these things" (Rev. 4:1 NASB).

"And they heard a loud voice from heaven saying to them, 'Come up here.' Then they went up into heaven in the cloud, and their enemies watched then.'" (Rev. 11:12 NASB).

"And I saw heaven opened, and behold, a white horse, and He who sat on it {is} called Faithful and True, and in righteousness He judges and wages war." (Rev. 19:11 NASB).

You might be wondering why on earth I am sharing all of this with you. There is relevance today my friends. In Zechariah 3, Joshua the high priest was clothed in filthy garments, standing before an angel, and the angel said, "Remove the filthy garments from him." The angel declares the iniquity has been removed from Joshua and he is now clothed in festival garments and then a clean turban is placed upon his head.

Shortly after Dan and I were married, the Lord gave me a dream where I saw Dan on the corner of Randolph Road at Vail Avenue with a white turban on his head. I remember during that time period he was having severe headaches and went to the emergency room off Randolph Road to be checked out.

He spent 25 days in Mercy Hospital in 2012 just off Randolph Road on Vail Avenue. As I look back and see all the signs God was giving us for ministry and His warnings of things to come, it is quite amazing.

God was even showing me then how He would divinely intervene and I just didn't fully understand it. As God teaches us to connect the dots in life, we have greater understanding and can see His hand at work behind the scenes, sometimes when no one else can. God has a divine call on Dan's life. He has a plan for you too. Don't allow Satan to hinder your destiny through doubt, unbelief, fear, or your horrid past.

In Zechariah 3:7 Joshua is given charge to the Lord's court and **free access** to those standing there also. "Thus says the LORD of hosts, 'If you will walk in My ways and if you will perform My service, then you will also govern My house and also have charge of My courts, and I will grant you **free access** among these who are standing {here.} 'Now listen, Joshua the high priest, you and **your friends** who are sitting in front of you—indeed they are men who are a symbol, for behold, I am going to bring in My servant the Branch (Jesus)" (See Zechariah 3:7-8).

As Christians we have been granted free access to come boldly before the throne of God through Jesus Christ. What an amazing privilege. God opened our eyes to a new level of revelation at Mercy Hospital through the details and the Mercy Seat—where we have access through the blood of Jesus.

Paul wrote about this access to the Father by Jesus in Ephesians. "For through Him we both have our **access** in one Spirit to the Father" and "In whom we have boldness and confident **access** through faith in Him" (See Ephesians 2:18 and 3:12).

I believe God was showing me through the dream about the fountain of blood flowing from the Mercy Seat that He had an open heaven over us at Mercy for healing for Dan. This was a clear sign from God to encourage us to believe in Him and not to worry.

Remember earlier where I said the Lord spoke to my heart about hidden mysteries in God. He has mysteries for us today. It appears to me that the context of Daniel 12 is dealing with the times we are in right now.

I remember in January of 2008, the Lord whispered this to me, "After President Bush goes out and the new President comes in, then the end will come." We were planning a trip to India to host a Pastors' conference for 250 to 300 Pastors so I questioned the Lord about this. I asked Him why He was sending us to India a few months away. He said, "This will not start till January 21 of 2009." We can see the demise of America and other nations like never before in time across the world since that date. (Be sure to look for my next book coming out: IGNITE AMERICA)

The Book of Daniel was written for our time. In Daniel 12:9, we see Daniel is told to go his way for the words are sealed up until the end time. We can see in verse 3 that the Bible speaks of Christians who have divine insight and those who will lead many to righteousness and will shine brightly like the expanse of the heavens and the stars forever. (Take time to read Daniel chapter 12)

"Those who have insight will shine brightly like the brightness of the expanse of heaven, and those who lead the many to righteousness, like the stars forever and ever. But as for you, Daniel, conceal these words and seal up the book until the end of time; *many will go back and forth,* and knowledge will increase" (See Daniel 12:3-4).

CHAPTER 28

DIVINE INSIGHT

The Bible says, "But you, Daniel, keep this prophecy a secret; seal up the book until the time of the end. Many will rush here and there, and knowledge will increase" (Daniel 12:4 NLT)

"Many will go *back* and *forth*, and knowledge will increase."

I believe the Bible is speaking about believers who experience open gates, ancient doors or portals between the third heaven and earth. God is revealing much insight through His heavenly portals that is coming from angels descending to believers or believers ascending to heaven where we find knowledge increasing.

I remember being in a church service over 20 years ago and something specific the Lord spoke to a deacon to tell me. I mentioned this earlier in the book. The man had his wife tell me what the Lord had shown him. She said her husband saw my face in a ladder, in pain, but climbing higher to God—with angels ascending and descending on a ladder or staircase just like Jacob's ladder in the Bible. Her husband also told her to tell me not to ever let anyone pull me out of my walk with God—not even those who *purport* to be Christians.

God can teach us amazing things, when we listen. God still gives amazing revelation. He still reveals mysteries. God wants to open our eyes to divine insight and give us all hope again! He wants us to learn to live in God-confidence.

I believe God is revealing to us through Daniel 12:3-4 that in the last days He will raise up some believers who will bring much revelatory insight to the body of Christ and to the world for the harvest—the gathering in of saints and lost souls.

God has been revealing what is holding back revival from happening in churches, cities and regions, especially recently. He has been revealing the hearts of people and what He is seeing. I've been paying close attention to what He is showing me and pondering it in my heart.

When the gates of heaven open to people, they are taught such mysteries. I believe God is opening portals over individuals who will minister under an open heaven; those who have a heart for doing His will, not their own. I believe there will be individuals who will minister not only under an open heaven, but who will carry such a heavy anointing that wherever they travel miracles will happen and revival will break out for a gathering of the end-time harvest of souls. I sense God is preparing the stage for the greatest revival we have ever witnessed.

People are desperate. People who are desperate for God get His attention. When we experience open heavens, biblical understanding of God's Word comes, bringing clarity to the meaning and correction to any who have wrong thinking. This will come to those who are willing to accept truth. However, all will not.

Paul experienced great revelation as foretold by the prophet Daniel in chapter 12:3-4 and heard such inexpressible words that he *knew* he was not permitted to speak. Paul was caught up through a portal:

"I know a man in Christ who fourteen years ago— whether in the body I do not know, or out of the body I do not know, God knows—such a man was caught up to the **third heaven.** And I know how such a man—whether in the body or apart from the body I do not know, God knows **was**

caught up into Paradise and heard inexpressible words, which a man is not permitted to speak" (See 2 Cor. 12:2-4).

It seems to me that many are caught up in merchandising the anointing rather than spreading the gospel of Jesus Christ through the anointing. It takes money to do ministry. There is a business side of ministry. Jesus had followers that gave to His ministry. We know this as He had a treasurer. We must keep our focus on Jesus, the author and finisher of our faith.

God wants us to be caught up in His plan and purposes for the kingdom's sake. It is God's desire that none should perish. God is still transforming people today into the image of His dear Son.

Jesus touched the disciples and they looked up and saw no one but Jesus only. (See Matthew 17) Could it be we keep our focus on people and problems, rather than on Jesus? Jesus wants to touch your life today and tell you not to be afraid. Get your eyes on Him.

Please read Psalm 24:7 as it speaks of the King coming in or coming down through the ancient gate and again as Daniel 12:3-4 records "back and forth" of believers in the third heaven encounters. "Lift up your head, O gates, And be lifted up, O ancient doors, That the King of glory may come in!" (Psalm 24:7 NASB).

The Bible speaks of the believer entering in, "Open to me the gates of righteousness; I shall enter through them, I shall give thanks to the LORD. This is the gate of the LORD; The righteous will enter through it" (Psalm 118:19-20 NASB).

Don't seek experiences, but seek God with all your heart. I strongly believe it is by continually seeking Him, and being faithful, that portals may be established by God for His purposes and His glory.

I firmly believe God had established an open heaven over us at Mercy Hospital. I believe that is why He gave me the dream about the four sided plexi-glass machine with the fountain of purple liquid that flowed to the Mercy

Seat in Heaven through the clouds. Then when He spoke to my heart to sit on the rock and tree that is a beautifully sculptured piece of artwork, He spoke to my heart to check out the name first. I walked over to the small corner podium that had a bronze plate with inscription about the rock and tree named *"The Mercy Seat."* Could it be God is speaking to us more than most are aware? He always shows us in the natural what is going on in the spirit realm if we will just pay attention. God brought heaven to earth at Mercy Hospital for my husband Dan.

The fact that the LORD spoke to my heart that the *"son had gone before me"* as I walked the long hallway to the room where my husband was also no accident. It was the same hallway and the same exact room where our son lay seven years earlier being prepared for a heart catheterization. The LORD showed me the amazing truths found in being connected with Him as He walks with us and talks with us and shows us things to come. *The Son of God has gone before us to also prepare a place for you and I. What a hope we have in Jesus!*

When my daddy was seeing the lights on the field out the window at the hospital that my mother *could not see,* could it be that God had opened the heavens for Daddy to see his pathway to his eternal home? I know that when he first shared the vision with me, my heart sank and the first thing I thought about was the movie, "Field of Dreams" which made me realize Daddy was probably going to walk that field...home to be with his LORD.

The CD that I found strategically placed underneath our bed that had the song lyrics...*WALKING THE FIELD OF WHITE LIGHTS* was no accident. God was preparing us for the future and giving us time to understand. The fact that God didn't allow me to hear the first part of the CD until the week before Daddy died was not coincidental either... *COMING UP TO THE PLACE I DIE*...was no accident, but the love of God warning and preparing us for things to come.

Could it be we had to stay at Mercy Hospital for 25 days as the enemy was trying to block the answer to prayer the same way he did with Daniel when he prayed for 21 days in the Bible? Could it be that God was allowing us to be divinely positioned at Mercy *because* of His mercy so we could share this amazing story of His divine intervention?

Divine intervention still happens today. God has not changed! He is the Great I AM. His Word never fails and His compassions fail not. He is the same yesterday, today and forever! God wants to lead us out of bondage just like He had Moses lead the children of Israel out of Egypt to the fullness of operating in His power today as we can read in the book of Acts! The Bible is an up-to-date relevant book that is Truth for today.

Learn to enjoy each day with those you love. The future is not in our hands. God gives us day by day, breath by breath, to enjoy each day. He does not promise us tomorrow. Learn to live with your feet shod with the gospel of peace by abiding in Jesus. Live eternity-minded and remember, *there's no place like home—home with Jesus and the family of God.*

RUBY RED SHOES

The Lord gave me a dream I had on a pair of red shoes and was saying, "There's no place like home." Do you know where your eternal home will be? The most important decision you will ever make is to choose to follow Christ. The second most important decision is whom you marry. Live to know God and die to make Him known. I am not the same as I was ten years ago. I am not the same as I was twenty years ago. We are all a work in progress. If you are still alive, there is hope for you. Ask God to come into you heart if you have not already done so. Believe and receive His grace and mercy today.

Jesus is seated at the right hand of the Father and praying that your faith would not fail. The fountain that never runs dry is still flowing from the Mercy Seat in heaven! Thank God for the Mercy Seat and for the mercy God showed us at Mercy Hospital on Vail Avenue for twenty-five days in His loving care, tender mercy, and divine intervention that was strategically exhibited. He cares deeply for His children. He cares deeply for you. Don't waste another day of your life. Step into His plan for your life today. He still speaks and still divinely intervenes.

The Blood of Jesus still covers. His fountain of healing is flowing from the Mercy Seat to bring heaven to earth as we believe and plead the blood of Jesus. His blood still speaks.

"This will be a sign to you: You will find a baby wrapped in cloths and lying in a manger" —Luke 2:12 NIV

HEART CHECK

You may think it is strange that God resorts to signs to reveal Himself, but the Bible supports the fact that He does. The truth that God gives signs, like the stars that led wise men to Jesus, confirms how much we are loved and how desperately God is trying to communicate with us.

Pray and ask God to open your eyes of understanding and cause you to see the signs of the times. Ask God to give you His wisdom and understanding to discern them correctly.

Ask yourself this question: What is God trying to communicate to me?

Tell the LORD you don't want to miss anything He has to say or show you. You can also do a little research in your concordance or on the computer and look up the word *sign* in the Bible. You will be amazed at what you will learn.

CHAPTER 29

CONFESSION PRAYER

I speak faith. A good strong positive confession of God's Word changes your attitude. A positive confession of God's Word in prayer concerning favor with God and with man will put life into your spirit. You will begin to feel oppression leave and your faith will arise. The Lord is in the business of blessing you. He has great things planned in advance for you to do. He is a good Father. He makes His face to shine upon you. Begin to declare these things out of your mouth through daily confession.

Say it right now, "God loves me and favors me today. God honors me today and I am a success because every thing I put my hand to, God causes to prosper. He makes His face to shine upon me today. I live in divine health. I shall live and not die, and declare all the miracles of God and tell of His wonders (Psalm 118:17). The Lord is gracious to me today. I am very special to Him. My family is very special to Him. He makes every crooked place straight and brings me into a large place of abundance as I seek after Him and obey Him. God has chosen me, called me out, and is favoring me today in every area of my life. I love all people and all people love me. He connects me with others through divine connections for His purposes.

I am being filled with the fullness of God. The power of the Holy Spirit is at work in me, I am being rooted and grounded in the love of God. God is doing exceedingly abundantly above all that I ask or think. His mighty power is strongly at work in me and leads my every step. With God, nothing is impossible (Luke 1:37). I ask the Holy Spirit to put a guard over my mouth that I would not sin against the Lord through speaking negatively about myself, my circumstances, my family, business, ministry, relationships and others.

I am blessed and highly favored and I am a success. I am flowing in God's love, and others are being blessed through my life and ministry. I am releasing God's miracle power in my life, I am receiving healing, and others are receiving healings, both in mind and body, through my words and ministry.

I am excited and expect God to do great things. I can't wait to see what God has planned today. No matter what my circumstances, I give God praise and know that nothing is impossible with Him. I command my body to line up with the Word of God and operate the way God created me and formed me in my mother's womb. I am an overcomer by the blood of the lamb (Jesus Christ) and the word of my testimony. I have radical faith. I step out in obedience in childlike faith at the slightest whisper from God. The faith of God is in me. His life is in me. I can do things I never dreamed of because I trust God and He has provided all I need. He has provided all we need for our family.

Lord, I ask You to bless my enemies and those who have wronged me. I speak peace and order where there is confusion and chaos. You are not the God of confusion. Because I am a child of the Most High King, may the Lord rebuke Satan in every area of my life. Because I tithe and am a giver (based on Malachi 3), the Lord rebukes Satan in every area of my life.

I am free to live in Christ because He lives in me. I am a new creation with amazing talents and gifts to be used by God as a servant of His for His glory. I expect great things from God and He turns all things out for my good, and His glory. The truth makes me free. ("The truth makes you free," declared the Lord in John 8:22). God is pouring out His spirit of favor upon me today because of His great love. I do not accept defeat. God is the lifter of my head. He is the Great I AM. He is everything I need for today and tomorrow. He never changes. I am faith-filled and have the divine favor of God operating in me and through me today and forever. I live in the favor of God for life. I love God and choose to love others. God loves me extravagantly. I live in His divine river of blessings and life because Jesus is seated at the right hand of the Father, interceding for me that my faith would not fail.

I love you Lord and I lift my voice to praise you and say what You say about me and my family, my friends, my business and I give you praise for what you are going to do today.

I confess: "I grow in spirit and strength, I wax strong in spirit, I am being filled with wisdom; and the grace of God is upon me and my family" (based on Luke 2:40). I confess this over my family and children and grandchildren as well.

In Jesus name,

Amen!

"Bless the LORD, you His angels, Who excel in strength, who do His Word, Heeding the voice of His word." —Psalm 103:20 NKV

HEART CHECK

Ask yourself this question: How did I feel when I prayed this?

When we pray the Word of God out loud and make

positive confessions, angels hearken to the *voice* of the Word of God and move into action to bring answers to prayer. Don't allow the enemy to make you doubt or stay in unbelief another day. Begin to say what God says about you!

CHAPTER 30

MIDNIGHT CRY

America needs hope again. As a nation, we need to cry out to God like we are in a life or death situation as Dan experienced. We need to run daily to the Mercy Seat and seek God like never before.

Similarly to my husband's heart issues, I believe America, as a nation, has a heart problem. The world has a heart problem. America was founded on God but is in serious trouble. It seems that hearts in America have become hardened and calcified due to desensitization across our once great land.

Could it be that our founding forefathers would croak at what they would see today if they were still alive? They might have a heart attack themselves. Many of our young people today are wandering through their teenage years trying to figure life out, what it's all about, why they were born, and whether they are saved or unsaved. Fathers have abandoned children. Mothers have abandoned children. Children are turning on their own parents in life and business. Thousands have been aborted. What on earth is wrong in America and other nations?

Whether it is the teenagers in your own home to the young people in your church, whether it is the neighborhood teens or your children's friends, instead of just leaving them in the dark or the cold, don't you think it is wisdom to encourage them, mentor them and coach them so they are not like the rest of the world? In a world of despair, they can get the idea they are losers and never figure out what to do with their own life or even have hope of a career.

With the extreme amounts of debt, to the lack of hope that is broadcast on every form of media, to the rejection and bullying issues even through social media, one can lose all hope. Families are moving due to loss of jobs, homes, and massive amounts of debt. Children and parents are in transition in every area of life, it seems.

As a child, I never had to deal with the kind of issues the world faces today. Spit wads and chewing gum were the two issues when I was in school. Since prayer was taken out of schools—America has changed, and not for the better.

Little kids are prone to hide and do things in fear or cover things, but they are born with a nature to know right and wrong. Even one of our grandchildren, Logan, is really cute the way he eats Hershey's Kisses and hides them under our cat's bed.

The next time Logan came over, I explained to him he could have as many chocolate Hershey Kisses as he wants as long as he always asks first and throws the wrappers away in the trash. Finding the little silver wrappers was like finding a silver lining in a cloud. Our cat, Hobbs, had recently died so God used the little silver wrappers to make me smile at what Logan had done. It made me laugh and chuckle at the nature of little children.

Adults hide and cover up things as well. Children can get taller and become adolescent adults with no sense of responsibility but a desire to achieve with someone else paying the cost. Welcome to America. It is not the children's fault—it is the responsibility of parents. The last generation has given too much and has enabled the next to have a spirit of entitlement, without a cost.

Madison Avenue and Wall Street have attempted to capture the hearts of people to the point of deception—preparing to sell them anything they can, trying to capture youth while they are young, and making people think they can get rich quick to the point of tragedy. If you have your hope in Wall Street, it will become *WORTHLESS AVENUE.*

I remember several years ago, the Lord spoke something to my spirit in a dream when I was asleep. It actually woke me up. We were on a business trip in New York City. This is what I heard: "Wall Street is Worthless Avenue." Two days later, the stock market hit an all-time low. God was showing me things to come and then confirmed it as well in the natural. This is how He trains us.

If you have your hope in anything other than God, you are already in trouble. America needs heart surgery. When you hear of the broken homes, families and teens on drugs and alcohol, to the lonely women filling the bar scenes, and the men having affairs on their wives and destroying their careers and family, it is a tragedy.

We cannot be like the priest and the Levite who walked by the man who was robbed because of being busy and uncaring. We must choose to be like the Good Samaritan and make a difference. There is hope in God and it is time to *stand up, raise a standard and get our hope back in GOD!*

The good news is we can do something to help—we can love God, love people and pass it on. We can choose to care and capture the hearts of our neighbors and the hearts of this generation before the world does.

You can spend your entire lifetime searching the depths of truth about God and the gospel of Jesus Christ. The fundamental standard and measure of God's truth and Satan's lie is summed up in what Jesus asked Peter: "Who do men say that I am?" Some will say Jesus is a prophet, some say He is a great teacher, or martyr, but Peter got it right: **"You are the Christ, the Son of the living God" (Matt. 16:16 NASB 1984).**

The person of Jesus Christ is the standard by which everything is measured. Satan hopes to get as many people to follow after him and his ways, but in the end they will find themselves deceived.

The power of the gospel is the person and work of Jesus Christ. His power is active today—and was made evident through all the divine interventions at Mercy on Vail Avenue. Don't allow the enemy to veil your eyes to the truth.

Jesus died for our sin. The blood Jesus shed on the cross was a guilt offering for the sins of every person. Forgiveness and righteousness are offered to every person who by faith in His name receives these gifts.

The Bible says, "Surely the arm of the Lord is not too short to save, nor his ear too dull to hear. But your iniquities have separated you from your God; your sins have hidden his face from you, so that he will not hear" (Isaiah 59:1-2 NIV)

The Good News is this: our separation and guilt are removed. Jesus, the perfect lamb without sin, gave Himself as our sin offering. Jesus Christ died and rose from the dead. His resurrection power is still at work today. Jesus brought Lazarus back from the dead. He raised my husband back up and saved him from early death.

Jesus was resurrected with a glorified body and he lives forever. That is the same thing that happens to all who accept, believe and receive Him as Lord and Savior. All judgment and authority have been given to the Son, Jesus Christ. When the world as we know it is over, it will not be the Father who will judge the world. He has assigned that privilege to His Son.

The Bible says--For he has set a day when he will judge the world with justice by the man he has appointed. He has given proof of this to all men by raising him from the dead. (See Acts 17:31)

Our standard is Jesus Christ. The power of the gospel is the person and work of Jesus Christ. We must turn our focus to Him! I call it an upward gaze.

The Church must arise and get back to the basics. With our help, people can discover early in life what they were born to do and have a glimpse of their potential that God has given them. We as parents, grandparents and leaders can encourage the next generation to soar to new heights like an eagle and have hope again in God! It is time we had a midnight cry like Paul and Silas in jail.

Paul and Silas did suffer some persecution well before midnight, but so have many of us. This is the time for wise and foolish groups to both "awake" and get out of their lethargic apathy and live to honor Christ. Could it be God is waking us all up to give us hope again? The enemy targets anyone who is a threat to the kingdom of darkness. He also targets children and youth, as they are the next generation of leaders.

I am sure we have all had times of attack and thought the sun might not ever come up again; maybe for weeks after the death of a spouse, loss of home, career, or diagnosis of a debilitating disease. Perhaps, it was when your father died and a week later your mother had a stroke and was found on the floor three days after it happened. Whatever the case, God still cares and there is hope in Him!

Don't allow Satan to build a wall of doubt or an inner prison of suffering in your life as a child of God. The best sermon you may ever preach is *HOPE IN GOD*. Your life is an example of either *hope in God* or hope in self. Self-confidence is an inward glance while God-confidence is an upward gaze. Where is your hope?

We can live with such transparency and a leap of faith in God that this generation sees it is possible to triumph over the world. Jesus Christ, the sinless specimen of humanity who best demonstrated the unlimited nature of potential in mankind, said, *EVERYTHING IS POSSIBLE FOR HIM WHO BELIEVES* (Mark 9:23 NIV).

Don't allow fear to cripple you beyond hope. *Fear of*

*man will prove to be a snare, but whoever trusts in the Lord
is kept safe.* (Proverbs 29:25 NIV)

Jesus shed His precious blood for you and I. There were
seven places He shed His blood—His head, in the Garden of
Gethsemane, His beard and face, His head, from the crown
of thorns, His beaten back, His hands, nailed to the cross,
His feet, as the nails were driven in and His pierced side.

This was the greatest act of the Father's love for you and
me. The greatest demonstration of the Father heart of God
seems to come with His attention to the details in our life. He
surprises us with extra things—little pleasures and treasures
that only a father would know we need or would like. He
goes to extreme measures to show *HIS GREAT LOVE* on
behalf of His children.

God is not materialistic nor is he stingy. People use
people to get things. God uses things to bless people. Don't
you think it is time we put our hope back in God—before it's
too late?

Let's apply hope to our lives again. The Bible says,
"Charity [agape faith] suffereth long, and is kind; charity
envieth not; charity vaunteth not itself, is not puffed up,
Does not behave itself unseemly, seeketh not her own, is not
easily provoked, thinketh no evil; Rejoiceth not in iniquity,
but rejoiceth in the truth; Beareth all things, believeth all
things, hopeth all things, endureth all things" (1 Corinthians
13:4-7 KJV).

Take a look at yourself in the mirror of God's Word and
ask yourself, "Do I see the best in every situation? Am I
constrained by the love of God to see the potential in other
people through the eyes of God's love or do I view them
with criticism and doubt?" Love believes the best!

The phrase "believeth all things" could be translated—
Love expects the best and simply believes God for the
very best in every situation. In the Sparkling Gems From
the Greek (by Rick Renner) we find the Greek word for

"hopeth" is the word *elpidzo,* which depicts not only a *hope,* but *an expectation of good things.* This means that rather than assuming failure or a bad result in someone's life, the *agape* love of God always expects the best in someone else. It not only expects it, but it is filled with an *anticipation* to see the manifestation of the thing hoped for. (See Sparkling Gems – page 685)

The phrase "hopeth all things" could be taken to mean— Love always anticipates the best in others and expects the best for others.

The word "endureth" is the Greek word *hupomeno.* It is the word *hupo,* which means *under,* and the word *meno,* which *means to stay* or *abide.* Rick Renner says, "compounded together, it depicts the attitude of *a person who is under a heavy load but refuses to surrender to defeat because he knows he is in his place."* We were at this place in Mercy Hospital, but refused to give into defeat and despair. We hoped beyond all hope in Jesus Christ, our blessed hope. He is our ONLY hope. We chose to stay put, abide in God's Word and refused to throw in the towel.

You see, God's love, His agape love never quits, never surrenders, and never gives up! Have you? Put your hope in Christ! Apply hope to your circumstances. Apply hope to your teens today. Apply hope to your marriage, business, health, or finances. Perhaps it is a fact you are having problems today, but there is still hope! Have hope again as an individual and let's have hope again as a body of believers in Christ for America, the nations and the next generation! Leave a legacy of hope in Christ. He is still performing miracles and He still speaks today.

HEART CHECK

"I will give you a new heart and put a new spirit within you; I will take the heart of stone out of your flesh and give you a heart of flesh. I will put My Spirit within you and cause you to walk in My statutes, and you will keep My judgments and do *them.*"—Ezekiel 36:26-27 NKJV

Ask the Lord to soften the hard places in your heart where you have become hardened and calloused. Much like a well, one must dig deeper to get through the stones to find fresh water. In the life of a believer, we must continually dig deeper and desire to know God more intimately.

Ask God to give you compassion for the spiritually wounded and dying.

Ask God to help you to slow down to hear Him and to recognize obstacles might be God's way of giving you a divine encounter.

CHAPTER 31

THE SPIRIT OF GOD
BRINGS REVELATION

On the day of Pentecost, seven weeks after Jesus' resurrection, the believers were meeting together in one place. Suddenly, there was a sound from heaven like a roaring of a mighty windstorm in the skies above them, and it filled the house where they were meeting. Then what looked like flames or tongues of fire appeared and settled on each of them. And everyone present was filled with the Holy Spirit and began speaking in other languages, as the Holy Spirit gave them this ability. (Acts 2:1-4 NLT)

Peter preaches to a crowd and tells them to make no mistake about what happened because what happened was predicted by the prophet Joel centuries ago.

The Bible says: "In the last days, God said, I will pour out my Spirit upon all people. Your sons and daughters will prophesy, your young men will see visions, and your old men will dream dreams. In those days I will pour out my Spirit upon all my servants, men and women alike, and they will prophesy" (Acts 2:16-18 NLT).

The Bible also tells us to respect people in authority in 1 Peter 2:13-17. We are to honor those in authority—fear God, show respect for everyone, love our brothers and sisters in Christ, and show respect for those in charge.

The Book of Revelation says: "He who has an ear, let

him hear what the Spirit is saying to the churches (see Rev.
2:7). God still speaks to those who listen. God will show you
things to come. The Lord began speaking some things to me a few nights
ago. I will share some with you. In Mark 16:15, we find
three reasons two-thirds of the name of God is, "GO!" The
Bible is simple. God knows everything about us and loves
us anyway!

He also knew we would analyze everything if He made it
more complex. He kept it short and simple. Jesus said, "Go"
because He has chosen to use people in His plan. He uses
us as His hands and feet in the earth to witness and win the
world. We obviously cannot win the world without Him. To
think so is actually foolishness.

God has made us participants in His plan. Whose plan?
That's right, God's plan. Many would like to hide behind
tradition or the sovereignty of God, claiming that if God
wanted to win the world, He might as well do it Himself with
one wind of His Spirit. The revelation of Scripture shows us
that He requires our participation.

It is pretty obvious to me that God is not so picky as
He chose me. He chose you. He chose adulterers, deceivers,
harlots, murderers, and swindlers. You might be thinking,
"I've never committed murder," but I can assure you that
you most likely have murdered someone with your tongue or
in your heart. You may have slandered someone and pierced
a heart, intentionally or unintentionally.

On the day of Pentecost, the fire of God sat on each of
them. God uses the available and He is the one who qualifies
us. We don't qualify ourselves. The Holy Spirit empowers us
as we step out and obey His instructions.

I woke up hearing the Lord speak to me all through the
night, so I figured I might as well get up and write. I began to
think about the donkey that spoke in the Bible. The thought
came to me, "Well, no wonder! Jesus sat on a donkey so all

donkeys now have power to speak. If God used a donkey to get His point across, and He did, He can use you and me as well."

I also kept thinking about Saul in the Old Testament who had a call on his life but made wrong choices and died. Then, I began to think about Saul in the New Testament, whose eyes were opened to see spiritually and his name was changed to Paul. No one wants to die without fulfilling their life purpose. I don't really think people wake up one morning and decide to destroy their own lives. It can be a series of wrong choices and following the wrong people.

There is always hope in God when we turn to Him.

He wants us to mature and grow up in Him—in the likeness of His dear Son, Jesus. God did not say GROW into all the world, He said "go." The emphasis seems to be on the word "go." The disciples were not dignitaries or extremely intelligent men. They were just common people doing their own thing. Where the truth therein lies, you end up growing when you choose to get moving and go somewhere. You make a choice to go.

Truth left to theory remains in the realm of doubt. That is exactly why Jesus led the disciples on the Sea of Galilee to the other side, knowing they were headed into a storm. It only takes one storm to know you are not in control, and one storm to know who is—*God! Jesus is God! Jesus is the Word made flesh.*

Jesus has already gone before us. The Son of God has gone before you and I. He has taken that walk of Mercy, just for you and me. When Jesus said to "go," He was not saying goodbye. The command to "go" is connected to a promise: "And lo I am with you always, even to the end of the age!" (Matthew 28:20). He would not send you somewhere He had not been Himself.

I believe the reason Jesus told the disciples to go to the other side is simple. It is obedience. Obedience is the key. Jesus is always on the other side of your obedience. He is the *resurrection* and *life*. Blessing is always on the other side of obedience. Get moving. Run to the Mercy Seat—the Bible says Jesus is seated at the right hand of the Father, the Mercy Seat. We are seated in heavenly places with Christ Jesus when we are born-again! Are you truly born-again?

We have the gift of time. If you are reading this, you still have the gift of time. We are still in time—between the middle and end of an open-ended story with pages yet to be written with what Jesus is doing in this world and in our lives. The Holy Spirit came and sat on the people as they waited at Pentecost and we, as Christians today, must continue in our purpose. The failure of not allowing the Holy Spirit freedom to move as He wills has damaged the nature of our witness— as well as the experience of authentic *ecclesia*—the church that Jesus built and is still building.

I can assure you that you will never know how much you truly believe until you are faced with a life or death crisis that matters to you. I knew we were in a life or death situation with my husband and I am forever grateful to God for His power manifested for 25 days at Mercy—and continually.

HEART CHECK

Ask yourself these questions:

What would I do in a life and death situation?

How would I respond in a similar situation?

Are there any of God's laws, written in the Bible that I know I am not following? (If so, repent and accept responsibility. You must not only turn *from* sin, but you must turn *to* God.)

What is God revealing to me that I am ignoring?

Do I have the Spirit of God living in me?

Do I truly have an intimate relationship with God or do I just know *about* Him?

Read John chapter 3:1-9 and understand that just like Nicodemus, we can all receive a personal, life-changing Word from Jesus. Be honest about your troubled heart or situation. Nicodemus came to Jesus with a troubled heart. Deep down, he knew he did not know the answers to life's most important questions. Something was missing. If you desire to go after God, be honest about the questions that may be lurking inside your mind when you think about death, your family, about heaven, and about hell. These are the main questions in life.

CHAPTER 32

ABRAM TOOK A
LEAP OF FAITH

The Lord God said to Abram, "Leave your country, your relatives, and your father's house, and go to the land that I will show you. I will cause you to become the father of a great nation. I will bless you and make you famous, and I will make you a blessing to others." (Gen. 12:1-2 NLT)

Abram had to take a leap of faith and step out into the unknown. This took great courage. God Himself was calling Abram. Paul tells us we need to step out in faith like Abram that simply believes in childlike faith and moves to action in immediate obedience with courageous faith and confidence in God. Peter chose to believe God and took a leap of faith by immediately obeying and following Jesus.

Twice in the Gospels, Jesus gives an instruction to His disciples to do something they wondered about. In Luke 5, after going out in Simon Peter's boat to address the crowd that followed Him to Lake Gennesaret, He tells Peter to "launch out into the deep and let your nets down for a draft" (Luke 5:4 KJV).

Peter reminds Him that they had been fishing all night and had caught nothing. "Nevertheless, he says, "at Thy word I will let down the net." You probably already know the story. They caught so many fish the net actually broke and they had to call over another boat to help haul in the catch because the boats were in danger of sinking.

We need others. There is so much to do as a believer and there ought not be competition or envy between the brethren. In John 21, Jesus calls to Peter and John and the others, "have you caught anything?" They say no, so He tells them to drop their nets over to the other side. According to John, they didn't know it was Jesus, but they do it anyway. They also brought in an enormous haul. Both times, Peter is overwhelmed at the presence of the Lord: in John 21, as soon as John recognizes Him, Peter –who was perhaps naked (a fishermen's superstition), throws on his robe and leaps into the water. In Luke 5, he flings himself at Jesus' feet and says, "Depart from me, for I am a sinful man, O Lord!"

Two things happen when we have an encounter with God. We recognize our sin and our need of Him. We also recognize our need to run to Him. We also become transparent enough to share our story so others can know God too! We are also broken because we see our sin and know we have need of a Savior. We also become thankful to God for saving us, and he causes us to become naked and unashamed to share our testimony and the good news of the gospel.

RUNNING OVER

This morning, I called Oliver's name and I saw his body barreling over the fence at the gate outside our home. Oliver (Ollie) is our next-door neighbor's cat who loves to visit us. He runs over each time he sees or hears us open a door. It is almost like he waits and watches for us to even open the garage or return home from a trip.

As I said, he heard my voice and took a leap of faith over the gate. Dan went out to give him treats and Ollie went to rest under a patio chaise. I went to the door again and slightly opened it. He immediately rose to a higher level and sat at the doorstep, waiting for another word and another open door. Actually, he was waiting for another treat and I sometimes pick him up and hold him close for a minute.

Sometimes I think cats have more sense than humans. Are you waiting to hear the next word from God and the next open door? Live with your eyes wide open in the Spirit realm and keep running to the Mercy Seat where the fountain never runs dry.

In our own personal lives, we can live with enough Word in us that we overflow to others. This morning I touched the button to make the coffee and smelled the fragrant aroma of Arabian coconut breeze coffee beans. Sadly to my surprise, I apparently had not noticed there was a little bit of coffee left in the pot. I cleaned out the top and when I checked, I thought Mother had already cleaned it out. Needless to say, it overflowed and I simply got to clean it up. It ran all down the cabinet and as I carried the coffee maker to the sink, it was still spilling on the floor.

As I think about it now, if we would each keep ourselves filled with the Word on a daily basis, we would still be overflowing the next morning. When you choose to keep running to the Mercy Seat, the throne of God in prayer, the Holy Spirit empowers you to live a life of grace and mercy to others. You will even have a better attitude. *Take a leap of faith today and begin to believe again. Live like Jesus may come today. Plan like you may live forever and dream huge dreams that only God can bring to pass. When we cooperate with Him, there are no limits to what He will do through our lives. Love others lavishly, give generously, forgive faithfully, and humbly submit each day to Him—Jesus, the Son of God!*

Are you able to take a leap of faith and realize you are clothed in the robe of righteousness? Do you know who you are in Christ? It is Jesus and what He did on the cross that is our covering. When we are born-again, God sees us through His Son and the finished work of the cross. We have to read the Word of God so the Holy Spirit can renew our minds daily.

Take time to read the Book of Hosea in the Bible. Hosea (name means Salvation) called out to Gomer (name means Beloved) and God is still calling out to you today. Hosea was married to an adulterer or harlot. God sees us through the Son and sees what He has designed us to be. He goes to extreme measures for the saving of the lost and to divinely intervene through the days of our lives. He is amazing and His love never fails.

It takes a leap of faith to be saved—but Jesus is calling us to live in His miracles daily by continually pursuing Him, and by chasing after the risky, ongoing, extravagant way of living in childlike faith to hear and obey Him immediately. When we take a leap of faith and partner with God, miracles become a way of life! I thank God for the miracles in my precious husband's life. What an amazing testimony to the power of God! Thank God for His mercy and grace that are new every morning and that can run over to others through our lives.

CHAPTER 33

THE MIRACLE AT CHRISTMAS

When Dan and I first started dating, I remember vividly what God did that is yet another miracle. It was Christmastime and I had already purchased him a nice leather Bible. I remember the day he asked me if we could go to the Christian bookstore to buy his daughter and her husband one for their wedding day. I was also going to pick up the Bible I had purchased for him as a gift because it was being engraved with his name.

As we walked into the store, I remember Dan saying we should buy one that was indexed for his daughter and it made me ask him a question. I asked him if he were buying one for himself, would he want it indexed or did it matter. He told me "definitely indexed" and my heart sank. I recall as if it were yesterday walking to the register to pick up my prepaid merchandise. I glanced down and saw a basket full of Afghans and one in particular stood out to me. Here is what I saw, "Delight yourself in the Lord, and He will give you the desires of your heart" (Psalm 37:4 NIV). The verse was stitched into the fabric beautifully. We left the store and came back to my house after we had finished shopping and had eaten dinner. After he left, I went into my bedroom to write in his Bible. I remember tears streaming down my face as I wrote a note in it to him and wrapped it in Christmas paper. I placed it under the tree and went to bed.

On Christmas morning, Dan came over early so we could open gifts. I gave him the other presents first and then saved the Bible for last. Just before he opened it, I explained it wasn't exactly perfect and told him the story. He removed the bow and opened the box. When he took the Bible out, God had supernaturally changed it from non-indexed to an indexed version—that was our first Christmas miracle. That is the love of God, my friends.

No, the bookstore did not switch the Bible on me. I brought the non-indexed Bible and wrote a Christmas message in it. God saw my desire and changed the Bible just like Psalm 37:4 says--it was as simple as Jesus turning the water to wine in John chapter two. With God, all things are possible. Do you believe?

Miracles are all around us. We just need a heart that is receptive, ears that hear and eyes that see! May God bless you with the desire of your heart as you seek Him, stand in the gap in prayer for your friends, family and all that you meet that do not know Him. Knowing God and making Him known should be your mission.

HEART CHECK

Ask yourself this question:

Do I believe in miracles?

God parted the Red Sea, transforms lives and is still doing it today. If you have doubt, Satan has clouded your view and your receptors. Ask God to renew your mind.

CHAPTER 34

PERSONAL ATTACK

David describes something every follower faces at some point in life in Psalm 38. We could have chosen to become discouraged with all we were facing, but instead we chose to trust God.

David was plagued with a spirit of discouragement. No Christian brings it on himself, nor does the Lord send it. Discouragement comes straight from the pit of hell. Satan hates believers and tries to convince us that God's wrath is upon us because we don't measure up to God's standards.

Paul urges us not to fall prey to this mental attack: "Lest Satan should get an advantage of us: for we are not ignorant of his devices" (2 Corinthians 2:11 KJV). Satan wants you to doubt and reason. He obviously knows he can't turn you away from Jesus, so he tries to make you depressed, discouraged and lose all hope. That's where some Americans live today.

There is hope in Jesus. After reading the accounts of God's divine intervention in my husband's life, you must know God cares for you too! We need Jesus and we all need a spiritual awakening, both personally and as a nation.

Don't get caught in the trap of trying to maneuver your way out of whatever you are facing. Instead, look to Jesus. There is conflict in the spiritual realm for your life and resources. We can talk to God about everything. He graciously invites us to come to Him and never wants us to even entertain the thought that He has abandoned us. Even in David's despair, he cried out: "For in thee, O Lord, do I hope: thou wilt hear, O Lord my God" (Psalm 38:15 KJV).

Jesus is our ONLY hope, and He is the source of life. Jesus is the answer to every problem we face in America. Jesus is the answer to every problem the world is facing. Let's take a look at what the Bible says in Psalm 42. David starts this out by expressing his deep thirst for the Lord: "As the hart [deer] panteth after the water brooks, so panteth my soul after thee, O God. My soul thirsteth for God, for the living God: when shall I come and appear before God?" (Psalm 42:1-2 KJV). We can see that David was pleading for a revelation from the Lord. His soul was cast down, but he never loved God more.

You may not *feel* like saying even one more prayer. You may be physically and mentally exhausted from physical or financial attack, and be discouraged beyond all natural hope—but there is HOPE IN JESUS. He is our ONLY hope! Go to prayer, allowing the Holy Spirit to do his work as you can see from this real life story of God's divine intervention. Dare to believe in God. Dare to believe the incredibly good things the Holy Spirit is going to tell you.

The Bible says, "As it is written, Eye hath not seen, nor ear heard, neither have entered into the heart of man, the things which God hath prepared for them that love him. But God hath revealed them unto us by his Spirit: for the Spirit searcheth all things, yea, the deep things of God" (1 Corinthians 2:9-10 KJV).

God sent His Spirit to comfort us, strengthen us and reveal the mind of Christ to us. Dare to believe and hope again. Take *a leap of faith* today! It's not too late!

It seems more people are losing hope and finding themselves overwhelmed with life circumstances. Problems are ever increasing with trials and tribulations on the rise. Let's believe like Abraham as Romans 4:18 tells us. "IN HOPE HE BELIEVED AGAINST HOPE. THAT HE SHOULD *BECOME...*" Put your hope in Christ in every circumstance. Take a leap of faith and become free, alive and joyful!

Our Lord has a wonderful plan for the life of every child of His. No satanic attack can alter those plans. God knows the heartache, sorrows, struggles and pain we face each day—yet He also knows the glorious things He has planned for us. The work of the Holy Spirit is to encourage us. Our part is simply to believe and trust Him to fulfill what the Father God has sent him to do. Find a place of quiet and pray this prayer with me:

Lord,

I know you abide in me. I know You have sent your Holy Spirit to comfort and encourage me, strengthen me and reveal the mind of Christ to me. Lift me up and lead me in your path that You have chosen for me. I choose to believe again and put all my hope in You!

Amen.

The Bible says, "Beloved, think it not strange concerning the fiery trial which is to try you, as though some strange thing happened to you." The Holy Spirit will expose the lies of the enemy and will begin to teach you all things. (See John 14:26)

What we have walked through recently---is a step-by-step, second by second, intense operation of the Hand of God. Thank God for His strategic training where we learn to hear Him at the slightest whisper and obey instantly---for the saving of lives.

No matter what personal crisis you might be facing to the issues America faces as a nation, there is hope in the BLESSED HOPE! Our ONLY hope is Jesus Christ.

CHAPTER 35

FREEDOM IN CHRIST

STEPS TO FREEDOM IN CHRIST

1. Know that God loves you: "For God so loved the world that he gave his only Son, that whoever believes in him shall not perish but have eternal life" (John 3:16 NIV).
2. Acknowledge your sin. "For all have sinned and fall short of the glory of God" (Romans 3:23 NIV).
3. Turn away from sin. "Therefore do not let sin reign in your mortal body so that you obey its evil desires. Do not offer the parts of your body to sin, as instruments of wickedness, but rather offer yourselves to God" (Romans 6:12-13 NIV).
4. Accept that Jesus is the only way. "I am the way and the truth and the life. No one comes to the father except through me" (John 14:6 NIV). "Salvation is found in no one else, for there is no other name under heaven given to men by which we must be saved" (Acts 4:12 NIV).
5. Realize that Jesus paid the penalty for your sins. "But he was pierced for our transgressions, he was crushed for our iniquities; the punishment that brought us peace was upon him, and by his wounds we are healed. We all, like sheep, have gone astray, each of us has turned to his own way; and the Lord has laid on him the iniquity of us all" (Isaiah 53:5-6 NIV).

6. Receive Jesus as Savior. "Here I am! I stand at the door and knock. If anyone hears my voice and opens the door, I will go in and eat with him, and he with me" (Revelation 3:20 NIV). "Yet to all who received him, to those who believed in his name, he gave the right to become children of God" (John 1:12 NIV).

Get excited about what God has planned for you!

May God himself, the God of peace, sanctify you through and through. May your whole spirit, soul and body be kept blameless at the coming of our Lord Jesus Christ. The one who calls you is faithful and he will do it. **(1 Thessalonians 5:23-24 NIV)**

It will all start with a leap of faith. Why not take your own?

--Deborah Starczewski

DIVINE INTERVENTION
SUMMARY

We walk through the valley with Jesus holding our hands. We learn to depend upon Him minute by minute, second by second. Have you ever been there? We have personally just walked through a valley with the Lord manifesting Himself at every turn. He exhibited His love in amazing ways. We must each learn to hear, lean on, depend on, and obey the Holy Spirit when He whispers at the door of our hearts. Life and death stands in the balance. We are trained to recognize Him in small daily events so that when we hear Him, and perhaps question or attempt to reason, we have learned to obey Him even when it makes no sense to our natural minds.

Such times are vital to life and death. People's lives are at stake for all eternity. TIME IS NOW. This appeared on my Apple Mac laptop March 24, 2012. I saw emails on my computer with a stairway to Heaven on a tunnel of light in front of me on the screen. *For all of you MacBook Pro users, you know what was happening!* TIME IS NOW. Wow! Can you hear the sweet nudging of God? God is showing us TIME IS NOW for moving on with God. It is not a time to be a pew warmer in your local church.

Our wonderful Shepherd led us every single step of the way. It is almost mind-boggling. Gently, Dan and I actually passed through the valley of the shadow of death as he went into heart failure on the catheterization table at Mercy Hospital February 24, 2012 in the afternoon hours and was released on the first day of spring, March 20, 2012 after two open-heart surgeries and two small strokes. What a testimony of God's resurrection power to give hope and encouragement to all.

One divine intervention after another is what we walked through and experienced with Jesus at our side every step of the way. It is truly amazing when we think back about His goodness and tender mercies that fail not. He is so loving and kind. What an honor and privilege to be a child of the most High God and King. I don't know how anyone makes it without Jesus!

I was keenly aware of the urgency of each moment and felt like I could never relax. I had total peace but I sensed urgency on a daily basis! As death approached our door, God blocked the enemy from taking Dan home early through divine intervention. I thank God for the wisdom of the physicians He had in place and for every person that was used as an instrument for God.

We must realize, for the child of God, death is not an end but only a door to a higher way of living and a life of intimacy like we have never known before with Christ. Death is just a door opening into the hallway of light that leads to eternity with God. It is not something to fear, but merely an experience where one passes through on the path to the perfect life God desires for everyone. Everyone will not choose life, which is why we have to be known by love and share the gospel in our everyday life so others have the opportunity to see Him at work in us.

This period of time at Mercy was extended and lasted nearly a month, from February 24th to the first day of spring on March 20, 2012. Let's give thanks to God, for He is the Great Shepherd.

Psalm 23 (KJV)

1. "THE Lord *is* my shepherd; I shall not want.
2. He maketh me to lie down in green pastures; he leadeth me beside the still waters.
3. He restoreth my soul; he leadeth me in the paths of righteousness for his name's sake.
4. Yea, though I walk through the valley of the shadow of death, I will fear no evil: for thou *art* with me; they rod and thy staff they comfort me.
5. Thou preparest a table before me in the presence of mine enemies; though anointest my head with oil; my cup runneth over.
6. Surely goodness and mercy shall follow me all the days of my life: and I will dwell in the house of the Lord forever.

It is interesting to note that the sheep are primarily left alone with the Shepherd with intimate and extremely personal contact with him and obviously, as we just experienced, under His watchful eye with the most personal undivided attention every second of the day and night.

I can imagine what David must have felt as he penned this Psalm firsthand. When Samuel was sent by God to anoint David as king of Israel he was not at home with his brothers. He was tending his father's flock on the hills. Do you suppose David was an excellent writer because he spent so much time with the Lord and with the flock?

Just as the Shepherd knows all the dangers and difficulties for his sheep, God, our Great Shepherd, knows all the peaks and valleys we will ever encounter. David knew the country like the palm of his own hand. Never did he take the sheep where he had not been himself.

When the Lord whispered to my heart, "the son has gone before you"...I knew exactly what He was saying to me about this situation. With all the dangers that were ahead, God was reminding me He knew all about it. Just like the Shepherd tending the flock, God is fully prepared at all times to safeguard his flock and tend to them with excellent and strategic care in every circumstance.

I had an unusual calmness in my Spirit but an urgency to move at every whisper of God's voice to my heart. I have a whole new meaning to the word "watch" as Mother and I sat by Dan's side 18 nights and every day as well for nearly a month. God supernaturally sustained us with little sleep. Thank God for His watchful eye! He never slumbers nor sleeps.

The Lord gives us quietness and calm assurance that possesses our soul as we learn to trust Him on a daily basis, minute by minute. This is only brought about by the Holy Spirit and the almighty hand of God exhibited in our lives.

"I fear no evil, for you are with me." He was and is with us during every turn in life as He goes before us to make every crooked place straight. His love is amazing.

In the Christian life we speak of wanting to move onto higher ground with God or a higher level, yet often forget there are many great valleys and ravines to make it through first. Just like the Shepherds know the high country have winding paths that lead up the mountains, with deep ravines on either side, we too must "watch" for the ravines in life. These paths wind through the dark valleys just like we experienced at Mercy.

Even though Dan and I have walked through, yet another series of valleys, we did not die there, nor did we stop, we are walking through. We did not stop God's work even though we were in a valley. God opened our eyes to see the fields before us—the staff and other people at Mercy that we had the privilege of meeting. We began to give out books and chose to talk to people who were in their own life and death situations.

We all face disappointment in life, frustrations from situations, discouraging times, miscommunication, to dark questionable days, but we can all know we are in the hands of God and trust Him second by second each day—like we did and walked out of Mercy on the first day of Spring.

Jesus was led by the Holy Spirit into the wilderness where he fasted and prayed for 40 days with Satan there at every turn. What wilderness have you experienced or are you experiencing? As I reflect on all the time in Mercy, I remember asking God to extend Dan's life like he did for King Hezekiah. With tears streaming down my face, I sensed an unexplainable calm assurance and quiet confidence in my Heavenly Father's care. We were in our Abba Father's hands, even in the valley.

We must each come to this quiet conviction of an attitude of a quiet acceptance in every adversity and tragedy. This is what I call moving on to higher ground with God. Trusting God at this level simply makes life much easier to bear and enjoy, fully knowing God has our best interest at heart. We often find that it is in the valley where we find refreshing, even while walking through turbulent times. Our greatest troubles sometimes position us for our greatest victories. We are extremely thankful to God for the restoration of Dan's life at Mercy through God's divine intervention.

I experienced great solace from God Himself, fully knowing He was speaking to me and giving me instructions at every turn. Even though the days were filled with desperate circumstances, we walked through God's divine refreshment. It seems as though we each have been the center of God's attention as His watchful eye was on every detail. The Lord takes us into places like these, I believe, so we can learn the richest lessons in order for us to never be the same; so we become more like Him and have another testimony to share about God's goodness. *There is an unusual source of strength from God when we walk through dark valleys where His light is so bright we can't miss it. Others may not notice, but we can. Others will come to know as we share our story.*

BIBLIOGRAPHY

Renner, Rick, *Sparkling Gems from the Greek* (n.p.: Teach All Nations, Rick Renner Ministries). Recommended daily devotional.

Scholar's Library Gold: LOGOS Software System.

Strong, James, *The New Strong's Guide to Bible Words: English Index to Hebrew and Greek Words* (Nashville, TN: Thomas Nelson Publishers, 2008).

Strong, James, *The New Strong's Exhaustive Concordance of the Bible* (Nashville, TN: Thomas Nelson Publishers, 1990).

Vine, W.E. *Vines Complete Expository Dictionary of Old and New Testament Words* (Nashville, TN: Thomas Nelson Publishers, 1996).

Scripture quotations marked (NLT) are taken from the *Holy Bible*, New Living Translation, copyright 1996. Used by permission of Tyndale House Publishers, Inc., Wheaton, Illinois 60189. All rights reserved.

The Revival Study Bible, copyright 2010 by Armour Publishing Pte Ltd.

The Holy Bible, New King James Version, copyright 1982 by Thomas Nelson, Inc. All rights reserved.

ENDNOTES

Chapter 1

ADVERSITY, ATTACKS AND STANDING

1. Internet Online Dictionary, Merrian-Webster.

Chapter 2

THE WALK IN MERCY

1. Wikipedia/On-line dictionary.

Chapter 4

WE MUST GET IN AGREEMENT

1. Recommended reading: "The Harbinger" by Jonathan Cahn.

Chapter 6

THE FIELD OF WHITE LIGHTS

1. Hungry Live CD (phrase).

Chapter 8

THE CROSSOVER AT PROVIDENCE

1. Rick Renner, Sparkling Gems from the Greek.

Chapter 13

THE HOLY SPIRIT IS OUR GUIDE

1. Rick Renner, Sparkling Gems from the Greek (studies)
2. History of General Eisenhour and General Patton/ On-line studies

Chapter 14

SUBMISSION AND SURRENDER

1. Rick Renner, Sparkling Gems from the Greek.
2. Hebrew Greek Dictionary.

Chapter 15

GOD'S LINK

1. Website: Judaism 101 Hebrew Alphabet
2. www.teachinghearts.org

Chapter 19

SALVATION AND ANOINTING

1. The Revival Study Bible, NKJV Page 1385 (Mark 14:3-Oil of Spikenard).
2. (notes)

3. The Amplified Bible, NKJV.

Chapter 24

COOPERATING WITH THE HOLY SPIRIT

1. NIV Holy Bible, 1973, 1978, 1984 by The International Bible Society (2 Corn 4: 10-12).
2. Hebrew Greek Dictionary.

Chapter 25

IT IS FINISHED AT THE CROSS

1. Scholar's Library Gold: LOGOS Software System
2. God's Priceless Treasure, ISBN 978-1-61638-664-1 copyright 2011 by Deborah Starczewski.
3. The Revival Study Bible.

Chapter 26

LISTEN, OBEY, COMMIT AND LEAVE A LEGACY

1. www.afeyewear.com/include/library/escada_eyewear. aspx.
2. Life experiences as a Seer of God and researching Scripture.
3. Research from http://seerofgod.com

Chapter 27

LIVING SUPERNATURALLY IN THE NATURAL

1. King James Version, Cambridge Ed. (Hebrew-Greek).

Chapter 30

MIDNIGHT CRY

1. Rick Renner, Sparkling Gems from the Greek, Page 685.

ABOUT THE AUTHOR

D r. Deborah Starczewski is enthusiastic, down to earth, compassionate, and humorous. She impacts the lives of everyone she encounters. Deborah inspires others with wisdom, motivation, and hope in God with a strong gifting in the prophetic.

Having personally experienced heartache, pain, and rejection, Deborah understands the challenges that often accompany everyday life. She focuses on knowing God and exemplifying Him to others as she imparts truth through the Word believing that everyone has been created by God for a divine purpose. Her message is powerful and her testimonies of God's supernatural intervention are miraculous! She will inspire you to seek God for yourself as she shares her wisdom and insight into the heart of God. Her life experiences of redemption and restoration give hope to all. Deborah's compassion is founded in the heart of Jesus!

Deborah's real life experiences, though extremely painful, have given her the ability to identify with the hurting, brokenhearted and those who don't understand what on earth is going on in their lives. Out of her own personal encounters with Jesus, she formed two conclusions that will never change: first, that Jesus Christ is alive; second, that the Bible is a true, relevant, up-to-date book. What matters most to Deborah is seeing lives changed, hearts healed and destinies fulfilled for those who dare to dream and step out into God's plan for their life. Deborah tells you what the

Word says and encourages you to know God for yourself. Her message is real and life transforming. Be prepared to take a leap of faith and believe God for yourself.

Deborah founded Star Ministries, Inc., based on John 2:5: "Whatever He says to you, Do it" on April 21, 1998; and a nonprofit organization, Star National Outreach Worldwide, Inc., in 2008 based on Psalm 51:7 and taking the gospel to the nations. She earned her doctorate at Life Christian University. She has a heart for God and people. She is a teacher at her church, faculty at a local Christian University, author and speaker. She and her husband are both ordained ministers and have a heart for revival. They desire to facilitate unity in the Body of Christ by bridge building and networking among leaders of various streams and backgrounds. Praying for Israel is a burden of their heart, as Israel fulfills her role in the consummation of the ages.

Deborah and Dan have been married for 16 plus years with two children and four grandchildren in their blended family. Deborah believes we have all been created to be ministers, cleverly disguised in whatever sphere of influence we find ourselves.

To contact the author write:
Dr. Deborah Starczewski
Star National Outreach Worldwide, Inc.
P.O. Box 70
Cornelius, NC 28031
Email: Deborah@starministriesinc.com
www.starministriesinc.com